ISLANDS,
THE UNIVERSE,
HOME

ISLANDS,
THE UNIVERSE,
HOME

Gretel Ehrlich

VIKING

VIKING
Published by the Penguin Group
Viking Penguin, a division of Penguin Books USA Inc.,
375 Hudson Street, New York, New York 10014, U.S.A.
Penguin Books Ltd, 27 Wrights Lane, London W8 5TZ, England
Penguin Books Australia Ltd, Ringwood, Victoria, Australia
Penguin Books Canada Ltd, 10 Alcorn Ave., Suite 300, Toronto, Ontario, Canada M4V 3B2
Penguin Books (N.Z.) Ltd, 182–190 Wairau Road, Auckland 10, New Zealand

Penguin Books Ltd, Registered Offices: Harmondsworth, Middlesex, England

First published in 1991 by Viking Penguin, a division of Penguin Books USA Inc.

1 3 5 7 9 10 8 6 4 2

"Spring" and "This Autumn Morning" first appeared in *Antaeus*; "The Source
of a River" in the *Sierra Club Wilderness Calendar*, and "Summer" in *Harper's*.

Grateful acknowledgment is made for permission to reprint
the following copyrighted works:
Excerpt from "Winter Dawn" by Tu Fu from *One Hundred Poems from the Chinese*
edited by Kenneth Rexroth. Copyright © 1971 by Kenneth Rexroth. Reprinted
by permission of New Directions Publishing Corp.
Excerpts from "The Eclipse of the Moon" by Lu T'ung and "Impromptu" by
Meng Chiao from *Poems of the Late T'ang* translated by A. C. Graham (Penguin
Classics, 1965). Copyright © A. C. Graham, 1965.
Selections from *Genji Days* by Edward G. Seidensticker. Published by Kodansha
International Ltd. © 1978, reprinted by permission. All rights reserved.
Excerpt from poem by Saigyo from *From the Country of Eight Islands:
An Anthology of Japanese Poetry* edited by Hiroaki Sato and Burton Watson.
Copyright © 1981 by Hiroaki Sato and Burton Watson.
Reprinted by permission of Doubleday, a division of Bantam
Doubleday Dell Publishing Group, Inc.

Drawings by the author

LIBRARY OF CONGRESS CATALOGING IN PUBLICATION DATA
Ehrlich, Gretel.
Islands, the universe, home / Gretel Ehrlich.
p.   cm.
ISBN 0–670–82161–6
I. Title.
PS3555.H7218   1991
814'.54—dc20   91-50154

Printed in the United States of America
Set in Granjon
Designed by Oksana Kushnir

How hard to make ashes of the mind,
to still the body!

Sugawara no Michizane

ACKNOWLEDGMENTS

Special thanks to astronomer Roger Kanacke, who allowed me to observe with him
at the NASA Observatory on Mauna Kea,
Hawaii; to botanist and friend Gary Nabhan; Jan Timbrooke at the Santa Barbara
Museum of Natural History for her help
with Chumash; the naturalists and biologists at Yellowstone National Park; friend
and biologist Brendan Kelly; Leila Philip,
who traveled with me to Japan and interpreted for me; our friends in Japan—
Kanzaki-san, Raku-san, Sakuraba-san, and
many others—who welcomed us along the
way; and my editor, Dan Frank, for his
clarity and great patience.

Thanks also to teachers and friends
on the path: Takashi Masaki, Ray Hunt,
Allan Savory, Lilla Kalman, Frank Hinck-
ley, Will Hunter, Patrick Markey, Rusty,
Sam, Yaki, Slim, and, of course, Press.

A fellowship from the Guggenheim Foundation helped make this book possible.
Warm thanks.

CONTENTS

LOOKING FOR A LOST DOG 3

SPRING 11

THE SOURCE OF A RIVER 27

SUMMER 35

ISLAND 63

THIS AUTUMN MORNING 69

THE BRIDGE TO HEAVEN 89

HOME IS HOW MANY PLACES 127

ARCHITECTURE 151

THE FASTING HEART 163

ISLANDS,
THE UNIVERSE,
HOME

LOOKING FOR
A LOST DOG

The most valuable thoughts which I entertain are anything
but what I thought. Nature abhors a vacuum, and if I can
only walk with sufficient carelessness I am sure to be filled.

THOREAU

I started off this morning looking for a lost dog.
He's a red heeler, blotched brown and white, and
I tell people he looks like a big saddle shoe. Born at Christmas on a thirty-below-zero night, he's tough, though his
right front leg is crooked where it froze to the ground.

It's the old needle-in-the-haystack routine: small dog—
huge landscape and rugged terrain. I go one way, my husband the other. I walk and I listen. While moving cows
once, the dog fell in a hole and disappeared. We heard him
whining but couldn't see where he had gone. I crouched

down, put my ear to the ground, and crawled toward the whines.

It's no wonder human beings are so narcissistic. The way our ears are constructed, we can hear only what is right next to us or else the internal monologue inside. I've taken to cupping my hands behind my ears—mulelike—and pricking them all the way forward or back to hear what's happened or what's ahead.

"Life is polyphonic," a Hungarian friend in her eighties said. She was a child prodigy from Budapest who had soloed on the violin in Paris and Berlin by the time she was twelve. "Childishly, I once thought hearing had mostly to do with music. Now that I'm too old to play the fiddle, I know it has to do with the great suspiration of life everywhere."

But back to the dog. I'm walking and looking and listening for him, though there is no trail, no clue, no direction to the search. Whimsically, I head north toward the falls. They're set in a deep gorge where Precambrian rock piles up to ten thousand feet on either side. A raven creaks overhead, flies into the cleft, glides toward a panel of white water splashing over a ledge, and comes out cawing.

To find what is lost is an art in some cultures. The Navajos employ "hand tremblers"—usually women—who go into a trance and "see" where the lost article or person is located. When I asked one such diviner what it was like when she was in trance, she said, "Lots of noise but noise that's hard to hear."

Near the falls the ground flattens out into a high-altitude valley before the mountain rises vertically. The falls roar, but they are overgrown with spruce, pine, and willow, and the closer I get, the harder it is to see them. Perhaps that is how it will be in my search for the dog.

We're worried about Frenchy, because last summer he was bitten three times by rattlesnakes. After the first bite he walked toward me, reeled, and collapsed. His eyes rolled back, and he drooled. I could see the two holes where the fangs went in. They looked like little eyes spying on me. I was sure the dog was dying. He lay in my arms for a long time, while I crooned to him. My last rites, however, seemed to have had the opposite effect: he perked up suddenly, then gave me a funny look as if to say, "Shut up, you fool." I drove him twenty miles to the vet's house. By the time we arrived, he resembled a monster. His nose and neck had swollen as though a football had been sewn under the skin.

I walk and walk. Past the falls, through a pass, toward a larger, rowdier creek. The sky goes black. In the distance, snow on the Owl Creek Mountains glares. A blue ocean seems to stretch between, and the black sky hangs over like a frown.

A string of cottonwoods whose tender leaves are the color of limes pulls me downstream. I come to the meadow with the abandoned apple orchard. Its trees have lost most of their blossoms; I feel as if I had caught them undressed.

The sun comes back, and the wind. It brings no dog, but ducks slide overhead. An Eskimo from Barrow told me the reason spring has such fierce winds is so the birds coming north will have something to fly on.

To find what is lost; to lose what is found. Several times I've thought I was losing my mind. Of course, minds aren't literally misplaced; on the contrary, we live too much in them. We listen gullibly, then feel severed because of the mind's clever tyrannies. As with viewing the falls, we can lose sight of what is too close, and the struggle between impulse and reason, passion and logic, occurs as we saunter from distant to close-up views.

The feet move; the mind wanders. In his essay on walking, Thoreau said, "The saunterer, in the good sense, is no more vagrant than the meandering river, which is all the while sedulously seeking the shortest course to the sea."

Today I'm filled with longings—for what I'm not, for all the other lives I can't lead, for what is impossible, for people I love who can't be in my life. Passions of all sorts struggle soundlessly, or else, like the falls, they are all noise but can't be seen.

Now I'm following a game trail up a sidehill. It's a mosaic of tracks—elk and deer, rabbit and bird. If city dwellers could imprint cement as they walked, it would look this way: tracks overlap, go backward and forward like the peregrine saunterings of the mind.

I see a dog track, or is it a coyote's? I get down on my hands and knees to sniff out a scent. What am I doing? I entertain preposterous expectations of myself as when I landed in Tokyo, where I felt so at home I thought I would break into fluent Japanese. Now I sniff the ground and smell only dirt. If I tried and tried, would the instinct regenerate inside me?

The tracks veer off the trail and disappear. Descending into a dry wash whose elegant tortured junipers resemble bonsai, I trip on a sagebrush root, and look. Deep in the center, there is a bird's nest. Instead of eggs, a locust stares up at me.

Some days I think this one place isn't enough. That's

when nothing is enough, when I want to live multiple lives and have the know-how and guts to love without limits. Those days, like today, I walk with a purpose but no destination. Only then do I see, at least momentarily, that most everything is here. To my left a towering cottonwood is lunatic with bird song. Under it, I'm a listening post while its great, gray trunk—like a baton—heaves its green symphony into the air.

I walk and walk, from the falls, over Grouse Hill, to the dry wash. Today it is enough to make a shadow.

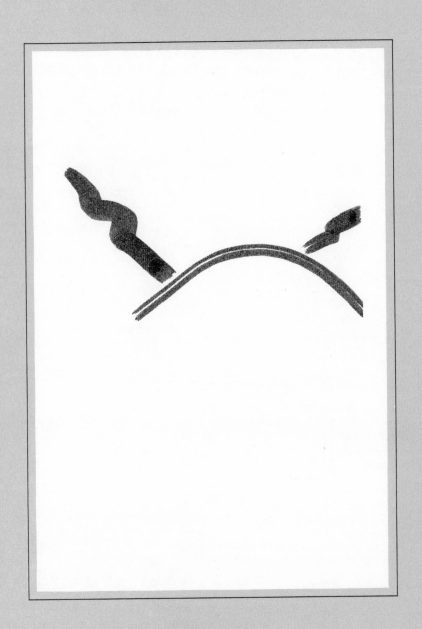

SPRING

We have a nine-acre lake on our ranch and a warm spring that feeds it all winter. By mid-March the lake ice begins to melt where the spring feeds in, and every year the same pair of mallards come ahead of the others and wait. Though there is very little open water, they seem content. They glide back and forth through a thin estuary, brushing watercress with their elegant, folded wings, then tip end-up to eat and, after, clamber onto the lip of ice that retreats, hardens forward, and retreats again.

Mornings, a transparent pane of ice lies over the meltwater. I peer through and see some kind of waterbug—

perhaps a leech—paddling like a sea turtle between green ladders of lakeweed. Cattails and sweet grass from the previous summer are bone dry, marked with black mold spots, and bend like elbows into the ice. They are swords that cut away the hard tenancy of winter. At the wide end, a mat of dead water plants has rolled back into a thick, impregnable breakwater. Near it, bubbles trapped under the ice are lenses focused straight up to catch the coming season.

It's spring again, and I wasn't finished with winter. That's what I said at the end of summer too. I stood on the ten-foot-high haystack and yelled, "No!" as the first snow fell. We had been up since four in the morning, picking the last bales of hay from the oat field by hand, slipping under the weight of them in the mud, and by the time we finished the stack, six inches of snow had fallen.

It's spring, but I was still cataloguing the different kinds of snow: snow that falls dry but is rained on; snow that melts down into hard crusts; wind-driven snow that looks blue; powder snow on hard pack on powder—a Linzer torte of snow. I look up. The troposphere is the five-mile-wide sleeve of air out of which all our weather shakes. A bank of clouds drives in from the south. Where in it, I wonder, does a snowflake take on its thumbprint uniqueness? Inside the cloud, where schools of flakes like schools of fish are flung this way and that? What gives the snowflake its needle, plate, column, branching shapes—the battering wind or the dust particles around which water vapor clings?

Near town the river ice breaks up and lies stacked in industrial-sized hunks on the banks—big as railway cars— and is flecked black by wheeling hurricanes of plowed topsoil. That's how I feel when winter breaks up inside me:

heavy, upended, inert against the flow of a new season. I
had thought about ice during the cold months too. How it
is movement betrayed, water seized in the moment of falling.
In November, ice thickened over the lake like a cataract
and from the air looked like a Cyclops: one bad eye. Under
its milky spans over irrigation ditches, the sound of water
running south was muffled. One solitary spire of ice hung
noiselessly against dark rock at the falls, as if mocking or
mirroring the broomtail comet on the horizon. Then, in
February, I tried for words not about ice but words hacked
from it—the ice at the end of the mind, so to speak—and
failed.

Those were winter things, and now it is spring, though
one name can't describe what, in Wyoming, is a three-part
affair: false spring, the vernal equinox, and the spring in
June, when flowers come and the grass grows.

Spring means restlessness. The physicist I've been talking to all winter says if I look more widely, deeply, and
microscopically all at once, I might see how springlike the
whole cosmos is. What I see as order and stillness, the robust,
time-bound determinacy of my life, is really a mirage suspended above chaos. "There's a lot of random jiggling going
on everywhere," he tells me. Winter's tight sky hovers. Under it, hayfields are green, then white, then green growing
under white. The confinement I've felt since November
resembles the confinement of subatomic particles, I'm told.
A natural velocity finally shows itself. Particles move and
become waves.

Sap rises in trees and in me, and the hard knot of
perseverance I cultivated to meet winter dissipates; I walk
away from the obsidian of bitter nights. Now snow comes

wet and heavy, but the air it traverses feels light. I sleep less and dream not of human entanglements but of animals I've never seen: a caterpillar fat as a man's thumb, made of linked silver tubes, has two heads—one human, one a butterfly's.

Last spring at this time I was coming out of a bout with pneumonia. I went to bed on January 1 and didn't get up until the end of February. Winter was a cocoon in which my gagging, basso cough shook the dark figures at the end of my bed. Had I read too much Hemingway? Or was I dying? I'd lie on my stomach and look out. Nothing close-up interested me. All engagements of mind—the circum-locutions of love interests and internal gossip—appeared false. Only my body was true. And my body was trying to close down, go out the window without me.

I saw things out there. Our ranch faces south down a long treeless valley whose vanishing point is two gray hills folded one in front of the other like two hands, beyond which is space, cerulean air, pleated clouds, and red mesas standing up like breaching whales in a valley three thousand feet below. Afternoons, our young horses played, rearing up on back legs and pawing oh so carefully at each other, reaching around, ears flat back, nipping manes and withers. One of those times their falsetto squeals looped across the pasture and hung, but when I tried to intone their sounds of delight, I found my lungs had no air.

It was thirty-five below zero that night. Our plumbing froze and because I was very weak my husband had to bundle me up and help me to the outhouse. Nothing close at hand seemed to register with me: neither the cold nor the semicoziness of an uninsulated house. But the stars were lurid. For a while I thought I saw dead horses, eating one another's manes and tails, spinning above my head in the ice fall.

Scientists talk animatedly about how insignificant we humans are when placed against the time scale of geology and the cosmos. I had heard it a hundred times but never felt it truly. Back in bed, I felt the black room was a screen through which parts of my body traveled, leaving the rest behind. I thought I was a sun flying over a barge whose iron holds soaked me up until I became rust, floating on a bright river. A ferocious loneliness took hold of me. That night a luscious, creamy fog rolled in like a roll of fat hugging me, but it was snow.

Recuperation is like spring: dormancy and vitality collide. In any year I'm like a bear, a partial hibernator. During January thaws I stick my nose out and peruse the frozen desolation as if reading a book whose language I don't know. In March I'm ramshackle, weak in the knees, giddy, dazzled by broken-backed clouds, the passing of Halley's comet, the on-and-off strobe of sun. Like a sheepherder, I x out each calendar day as if time were a forest through which I could clear-cut a way to the future. The physicist straightens me out on this point too. The notion of "time passing," like a train through a landscape, is an illusion, he says. I hold the Big Ben clock taken from a dead sheepherder's wagon. The clock measures intervals of time, not the speed of time, and the calendar is a scaffolding we hang as if time were rushing water we could harness. Time-bound, I hinge myself to a linear bias—cause and effect all laid out in a neat row.

Julius Caesar had a sense of humor about time. The Roman calendar with its kalends, nones, and ides—counting days—changed according to who was in power. Caesar serendipitously added days, changed the names of certain months, and when he was through, the calendar was so skewed, January fell in autumn.

Einsteinian time is too big for even Julius Caesar to have touched. It stretches and shrinks and dilates. Indecipherable from space, time is not one thing but an infinity of space-times, overlapping and interfering. There is no future that is not now, no past that is not now. Time includes every moment.

It's the Ides of March today.

I've walked to a hill a mile from the house. It's not really a hill but a mountain slope that heaves up, turns sideways, and comes straight down to a foot-wide creek. Everything I can see from here used to be a flatland covered with shallow water. "Used to be" means several hundred million years ago, and the land itself was not really "here" at all but part of a continent floating near Bermuda. On top is a fin of rock, a marine deposition from Jurassic times created by small waves moving in and out from the shore.

I've come here for peace and quiet and to see what's going on in this secluded valley away from ranch work and sorting corrals, but what I get is a slap on the ass by a prehistoric wave, gains and losses in altitude and aridity, outcrops of mud composed of rotting volcanic ash which fell continuously for ten thousand years, a hundred million years ago. The soils are a geologic flag—red, white, green, and gray. On one side of the hill, mountain mahogany gives off a scent like orange blossoms; on the other, colonies of sagebrush root wide in ground the color of Spanish roof tiles. And it still looks like the ocean to me. "How much truth can a man stand, sitting by the ocean, all that perpetual motion . . . ," Mose Allison, the jazz singer, sings.

The wind picks up and blusters. Its fat underbelly scrapes uneven ground, twisting toward me like taffy, slips up over the mountain and showers out across the Great Plains. The sea smell it carried all the way from Seattle has long since been absorbed by pink gruss—the rotting granite that spills down the slopes of the Rockies. Somewhere over the Midwest the wind slows, tangling in the hair of hardwood forests, and finally drops into the corridors of cities, past Manhattan's World Trade Center, ripping free again as it skims the Atlantic's green swell.

Spring jitterbugs inside me. Spring *is* wind, symphonic and billowing. A dark cloud pops like a blood blister, spraying red hail down. The sky widens, breaking itself. Wind concusses. It is a cloth that sails so birds have something to fly on.

A message reports to my brain, but I can't believe my eyes. The sheet of wind had a hole in it: an eagle just fell out of the sky as if down the chute of a troubled airplane. Landed, falling. Is there a leg broken? The sides of this narrow valley, a seashore 170,000 years ago, now lift like a medic's litter to catch up this bird.

Hopping, she flaps seven feet of wing and sways near a dead fawn whose carcass had recently been feasted upon. When I approached, all I could see of the animal was a rib cage rubbed red with fine tissue and the decapitated head lying peacefully against sagebrush, eyes closed.

Friends who have investigated eagles' nests have literally feared for their lives. An eagle's talons are a powerful jaw. Their grip is so strong the talons can slice through flesh to bone in one motion.

I had come close to seeing what was wrong, to seeing what I could do. An eagle with a bum leg will starve to death, but when I approached again she lifted her wings threateningly and, craning her neck, first to one side, then to the other, she stared hard, giving me "the eagle eye." Best to leave her alone. My husband dragged a road-killed deer up the mountain slope so she could eat, and I brought a bucket of water.

A golden eagle is not golden but black with yellow spots on the neck and wings. Looking at her, I had wondered how feathers—the rachis, vane, and quill—came to be.

Birds are glorified flying lizards. Positioned together, feathers are like hundreds of smaller wings, evolved from reptilian scales. Ancestral birds had thirteen pairs of cone-shaped teeth that grew in separate sockets like a snake's, rounded ribs, and bony tails. Archaeopteryx was half bird, half dinosaur, and glided instead of flying; ichthyornis was a fish-bird, a relative of the pelican; diatryma was a seven-foot-tall giant with a huge beak and with wings so absurdly small they must have been useless, though later the wing bone sprouted from them. *Aquila chrysaëtos,* the modern golden eagle, has seven thousand contour feathers, no teeth, and weighs about one pound. I think about the eagle on the hill. How big she was, how each time she spread her wings it was like a thought stretching between two seasons.

Back at the house, I relax with a beer. At 5:03 the vernal equinox occurs. I go outside and stand in the middle of a hayfield with my eyes closed. The universe is restless, but I want to feel celestial equipoise: twelve hours of daylight, twelve of dark, and the earth ramrod straight on its axis. Straightening my posture to resist the magnetic tilt back into dormancy, spiritual and emotional reticence, I imagine the equatorial sash, now nose-to-nose with the sun, sizzling like a piece of bacon, and the earth slowly tilting.

In the morning I walk to the valley. The eagle isn't there. The hindquarters of the road-killed deer have been eaten. Coyote tracks circle the carcass. Did they have eagle for dinner too?

Afternoon. I return. Far up on the opposite hill I see her, flapping and hopping to the top. When I stop, she stops and turns her head. Even at two hundred yards, I can feel the heat of her stare.

Later, looking through my binoculars, I try to see the world with eagle eyes. After glassing the crescent moon, I dream it has grown full and doubled. One moon is pink and spins fast; the other is an eagle's head, turning slowly in the opposite direction. Then both moons descend, and it is day.

At first light I clamber up the hill. Now the dead deer my husband brought is only a hoop of ribs, two forelegs, and hair. The eagle is not here or along the creek or on either hill. I climb the slope and sit. After a long wait she careens out from the narrow slit of the red-walled canyon whose creek drains into this valley. Surely it's the same bird. Flying by, she cocks her head and looks at me. I smile. What is a smile to her? Now she is not flying but lifting above the planet, far from me.

Late March. The emerald of the hayfields brightens. A flock of gray-capped rosy finches who overwintered here swarms a leafless apple tree, then falls from the smooth boughs like cut grass. The tree was planted by the Texan who homesteaded this ranch. As I walk past, one of the boughs, shaped like an undulating dragon, splits off from the trunk and drops.

Space is an arena where the rowdy particles that are the building blocks of life perform their antics. All spring, things fall; the general law of increasing disorder is on the rise. What is it to be a cause without an effect, an effect without a cause, to abandon time-bound thinking, the use of tenses, the temporally related emotions of impatience, expectation, hope, and fear? But I can't. At the edge of the lake I watch ducks. Like them, my thinking rises and falls on the same water.

Another day. Feeling small-minded, I take a plane ride over Wyoming. As we take off, the plane resists accepting air under its wings. Is this how an eagle feels? Ernst Mach's principle tells me that an object's resistance against being accelerated is not the intrinsic property of matter but a measure of its interaction with the universe; that matter has inertia only because it exists in relation to other matter.

Airborne, we fly southeast from Heart Mountain across the Big Horn River, over the long red wall where Butch Cassidy trailed stolen horses, across the high plains to Laramie. Coming home, we hit clouds. Turbulence, like many forms of trouble, cannot always be seen. We bounce so hard my arms sail helplessly above my head. In evolution, wing bones became arms and hands; perhaps I'm de-evolving.

From ten thousand feet I can see that spring is only half here: the southern part of the state, being higher in altitude, is white; the northern half is green. Time is one

of spring's greening forms, a clock whose hands are blades
of grass moving vertically, up through the fringe of numbers,
spreading across the middle of the face, sinking again as the
sun moves from one horizon to the other. Time doesn't go
anywhere; the shadow of the plane, my shadow, moves
across it.

To sit on a plane is to sit on the edge of sleep, where
the mind's forge brightens into incongruities. Down there
I see disparate wholenesses strung together and the string
dissolving. Mountains run like rivers; I fly through waves
and waves of chiaroscuro light. The land looks bare but is
articulate. The body of the plane is my body, pressing into
spring, pressing matter into relation with matter. Is it even
necessary to say the obvious? That spring brings on surges
of desire? From this disinterested height I say out loud what
Saint Augustine wrote: "My love is my weight. Because of
it I move."

Directly below us now is the fine old Wyoming ranch
where Joel, Mart, Dave, Hughy, and I have moved thousands
of head of cattle. Joel's father, Smokey, was one of two
brothers who put the outfit together. They worked hard,
lived frugally, and even after his brother died, Smokey did
not marry until his late fifties. As testimony to a long bach-
elorhood, there is no kitchen in the main house. The cookhouse stands separate from all the other buildings. In back
is a bedroom and bath, which has housed a list of itinerant
cooks ten pages long.

Over the years I've helped during roundup and brand-
ing. We'd rise at four. Smokey, then in his eighties, cooked
flapjacks and boiled coffee on the wood cookstove. There
was a long table. Joel and Smokey always sat at one end.

They were look-alikes, both skin-and-bones tall, with tipped-up dark eyes set in narrow faces. Stern and vigilant, Smokey once threw a young hired hand out of the cookhouse because he hadn't grained his saddle horse after a long day's ride. "On this outfit we take care of our animals first," he said. "Then, if there's time, we eat."

Even in his early twenties, Joel had his father's dignity and razor-sharp wit. They both wore white Stetsons, identically shaped. Only their hands were different: Joel had eight fingers and one thumb—the other he lost while roping.

Ten summers ago my parents and I visited their ranch. We drank homemade whiskey left from Prohibition days, ate steaks cut from an Angus bull, four kinds of vegetables, watermelon, ice cream and pie. Despite a thirteen-year difference in our ages, Smokey wanted Joel to marry me. As we rose from the meal, he shook my father's hand. "I guess you'll be my son's father-in-law," he said. That was news to all of us. Joel's face turned crimson. My father threw me an astonished look, cleared his throat, and thanked his host for the fine meal.

One night Joel *did* come to my house and asked if I would take him into my bed. It was a gentlemanly proposition—doffed hat, moist eyes, a smile grimacing with loneliness.

"You're an older woman. Think of all you could teach me," he said jauntily but with a blush. He stood ramrod straight, waiting for an answer. My silence turned him away like a rolling wave, and he drove to the home ranch, spread out across the Emblem Bench, thirty-five miles away.

The night Joel died, I was staying at a friend's farm in Missouri. I had fallen asleep early, then awakened suddenly, feeling claustrophobic. I jumped out of bed and stood in the dark. I wanted to get out of there, drive home to Wyoming, and I didn't know why. Finally, at seven in the morning, able to sleep, I dreamed about a bird landing on, then lifting out of a tree along a riverbank. That was the night Joel's pickup rolled. He wasn't found until daylight and died on the way to the hospital.

Now I'm sitting on a fin of Gypsum Springs rock, looking west. The sun is setting. What I see are three gray cloud towers letting rain down at the horizon. The sky behind these massifs is gilded gold, and long fingers of land— benches where Charolais cattle graze—are pink. Somewhere over Joel's grave, the sky is bright. The road where he died shines like a dash in a Paul Klee painting. But here it is still winter: snow, dry as Styrofoam when squeezed together, tumbles into my lap. I think about flying and falling. The place in the sky where the eagle fell is dark. Why does a wounded eagle get well and fly away? Why do the head wounds of a young man cut him down? Useless questions.

Sex and death are the riddles thrown into the hopper, thrown down on the planet like red and black hailstones. Where one hits the earth, makes a crater, and melts, perhaps a weed can germinate; perhaps not. If I dice life into atoms, the trajectories I find are so wild, so random, anything could happen: life or nonlife. But once we have a body, who can give it up easily? Our own or others'? We check our clocks and build our beautiful narratives, under which indeterminacy seethes.

Sometimes, lying in bed, I feel like a flounder with its two eyes on one side pointing upward into nothingness. The casings of thought rattle. Then I realize there are no casings at all. Is it possible that the mind, like space, is finite but has no boundaries, no center or edge? I sit cross-legged on old blankets. My bare feet strain against the backs of my knees. Just as morning comes and the indigo lifts, the leaf-lessness of the old apple tree looks ornate. *Nothing in this world is plain.*

"Every atom in your body was once inside a star," another physicist says, trying to humor me. Not all atoms in all kinds of matter are shared. But who wouldn't find that idea appealing? Outside, shadows trade places with a sliver of sun, which trades places with shadow. A Pacific storm blows in from the south like a jib sail reaching far out, backhanding me with a tropical gust. It snows into my mouth, between my breasts, against my shins. Spring teaches me what space and time teach me: that I am a random multiple; that the many fit together; that my swell is a collision of particles. Spring is music, a seething minor, a twelve-tone scale. Odd harmonies amass and lift up only to dissolve.

Spring presses harder and harder and is feral. The first thunder cracks the sky into a larger domain. Sap rises in obdurateness. For the first time in seven months, rain slants down in a slow pavanne—sharp but soft, like desire. I drive the highway that crosses the wild-horse range. Near Emblem a lone black stud horse trots across the landscape. He travels north, then turns in my direction as if coming to me. Now, when I dream of Joel, he is riding that horse and he knows he is dead. One night he rides to my house, all smiles and shyness, and I let him in.

THE SOURCE OF A RIVER

*I*t's morning in the Absaroka Mountains. The word *absaroka* means "raven" in the Crow language, though I've seen no ravens in three days. Last night I slept with my head butted against an Engelmann's spruce, and when I woke, it was a many-armed goddess swinging around and around. The trunk is bigger than an elephant's leg. I stick my nose against it. Tiny opals of sap stick to my cheeks where the bark breaks up, textured: red and gray, coarse and smooth, wet and flaked.

I'm looking for the source of the Yellowstone River, and as we make the day-long ascent from a valley, I think about walking and wilderness. We use the word "wilderness," but perhaps we mean wildness. Isn't that why I've come here, to seek the wildness in myself and, in so doing, come on the wildness everywhere, because after all, I'm part of nature too.

Following the coastline of the lake, I watch how wind picks up water in dark blasts and drops it again. Ducks glide in V's away from me, out onto the fractured, darkening mirror. I stop. A hatch of mayflies powders the air, and the archaic, straight-winged dragonflies hang blunt-nosed above me. A friend talks about aquatic bugs: water beetles, spinners, assassin bugs, and one that hatches, mates, and dies in a total life span of two hours. At the end of the meadow, the lake drains into a fast-moving creek. I quicken my pace and trudge upward. Walking is almost an ambulation of mind. The human armor of bones rattles, fat rolls, and inside this durable, fleshy prison of mine, I make a beeline toward otherness, lightness, or like a moth, toward flame.

Somewhere along the trail I laugh out loud. How shell-like the body seems suddenly—not fleshy at all, but inhuman and hard. And farther up, I step out of my skin though I'm still held fast by something, but what? I don't know.

How foolish the preparations for wilderness trips seem now. We pore over maps, chart our expeditions. We "gear up" at trailheads with pitons and crampons, horsepacks and backpacks, fly rods and cameras, forgetting the meaning of simply going, the mechanics of disburdenment. I look up from these thoughts: a blue heron rises from a gravel bar and glides behind a gray screen of dead trees, appears in an opening where an avalanche downed pines, and lands again on water.

THE SOURCE OF A RIVER

I stop to eat lunch. Emerson wrote: "The Gautama said that the first men ate the earth and found it sweet." I eat bologna and cheese and think about eating dirt. At this moment the mouth frames wonder, its width stands for the generous palate of consciousness. I cleanse my taste buds with miner's lettuce and stream water and try to imagine what kinds of sweetness the earth provides: the taste of glacial flour or the mineral taste of basalt, the fresh and foul bouquets of rivers, the desiccated, stinging flavor of a snowflake.

As I begin to walk again, it occurs to me that this notion of eating the earth is not about gluttony but about unconditional love, an acceptance of whatever taste comes across my tongue: flesh, wine, the unremarkable flavor of dirt. To find wildness, I must first offer myself up, accept all that comes before me: a bullfrog breathing hard on a rock; moose tracks under elk scats; a cloud that looks like a clothespin; a seep of water from a high cirque, black on brown rock, draining down from the brain of the world.

At treeline, bird song stops. I'm lifted into a movement of music with no particular notes, only windsounds becoming watersounds, becoming windsounds. Above, a cornice crowns a ridge and melts into a teal and turquoise lake, which, like a bladder, leaks its alchemical potions.

On top of Marston Pass I'm in a ruck of steep valleys and gray, treeless peaks. The alpine carpet, studded with red paintbrush and alpine buttercups, gives way to rock. Now, all the way across a valley, I see where water oozes from moss and mud, how, at its source, it quickly becomes a river.

Emerson also said: "Every natural fact is an emanation,

and that from which it emanates is an emanation also, and from every emanation is a new emanation." The ooze, the source of a great river, is now a white chute tumbling over brown bellies of conglomerate rock. Wind throws sheets of water to another part of the mountainside; soft earth gives way under my feet, clouds spill upward and spit rain. Isn't everything redolent with loss, with momentary radiance, a coming to different ground? Stone basins catch the waterfall, spill it again; thoughts and desires strung together are laddered down.

I see where meltwater is split by rock—half going west to the Pacific, the other going east to the Atlantic—for this is the Continental Divide. Down the other side, the air I gulp feels softer. Ice bridges the creek, then, when night comes but before the full moon, falling stars have the same look as water falling against the rock of night.

To rise above treeline is to go above thought, and after, the descent back into bird song, bog orchids, willows, and firs is to sink into the preliterate parts of ourselves. It is to forget discontent, undisciplined needs. Here, the world is only space, raw loneliness, green valleys hung vertically. Losing myself to it—if I can—I do not fall . . . or if I do, I'm only another cataract of water.

Wildness has no conditions, no sure routes, no peaks or goals, no source that is not instantly becoming something more than itself, then letting go of that, always becoming. It cannot be stripped to its complexity by CAT scan or telescope. Rather, it is a many-pointed truth, almost a bluntness, a sudden essence like the wild strawberries strung on scarlet runners under my feet. For half a mile, on hands and knees, I eat and eat. Wildness is source and fruition at once, as if this river circled round, mouth eating tail and tail eating source.

Now I am camped among trees again. Four yearling moose, their chestnut coats shiny from a summer's diet of willow shoots, tramp past my bedroll and drink from a spring that issues sulfurous water. The ooze, the white chute, the narrow stream—now almost a river—joins this small spring and slows into skinny oxbows and deep pools before breaking again on rock, down a stepladder of sequined riffles.

To trace the history of a river or a raindrop, as John Muir would have done, is also to trace the history of the soul, the history of the mind descending and arising in the body. In both, we constantly seek and stumble on divinity, which, like the cornice feeding the lake, and the spring becoming a waterfall, feeds, spills, falls, and feeds itself over and over again.

SUMMER

This June morning I walk north of our ranch, crossing two forks of the same creek split by three miles of mountain. At dawn there is no dew on the grass, and the wildflowers come and go in three weeks— an instant. Already this summer has been declared the driest since the dust bowl days of the 1930s. Scorching weather rarely felt here until mid-July has brought down what melt- water we have too soon and too fast for the earth to absorb. Hot, Mojave-like winds fill what are usually rainy days, and the native grasses are prematurely going to seed. Is someone holding a magnifying glass against the sun? Has the prediction that global warming was to have taken place in small increments been naive?

The sun inhales and exhales; its storms of heat reach down and strip the ground of memory, and the creek's split halves run meagerly, spending their drought songs in my ears, the one stream trying to hush the other. Above, two rock tablets, each the size of a five-story building, rise from the center of the steep mountain slope. Together they form an **M**, and a stain from an intermittent waterfall drives down through the center. As the sun rises, the rock catches light like a burnt shoulder.

I've come here looking for summer, as if the season were not a temporal occurrence but a geological one, a nugget of gold for which I could pan. I dive in and out of thick riparian vegetation, and only sudden openings, like green curtains drawn, allow me glimpses of water.

I'm looking for summer, but I can't find how or where it begins. Is it a prick of light, the spark from a horseshoe striking rock as I ride into the mountains? Can it be found in the green eruption of a leaf? It's my obsession, you see, to seek origins.

It's June twentieth, summer solstice, the longest day of the year and the hottest so far. Snow seems like something from another time, even though it snowed three feet in May. Now all that wavers in the mind is meltwater running fast, trying to get its rushing journey over with. At the moment the solstice occurs, my young saddle horse rolls in the dust, four legs in the air—motionless for a moment—and I run crouched like a thief out of the house through a hay meadow, over the tops of irrigation ditches, around the lake, through cattails, onto the thirty-foot-long island, all the time trying for a swift, gliding wolf gait in which the shoulders and head do not rise and fall but cut through air like a sword held out from the belly.

When the solstice is past, the sun is a flickering light behind fast-moving high clouds. As I step from the island into shallow, colorless water, three water snakes wind away in unison. Following deer who came to the lake to drink and returned to a nearby slope to graze, I sprint a quarter mile to the top of Mahogany Hill and turn north, my downhill foot slipping, my heart pumping forward to the end of an endless day. The sun finally goes at 10:00 P.M., only to rise again at 4:00 A.M.; but even without the sun the sky seems bright. That's how summer is: no past or future but all present tense, long twilights like vandals, breaking into new days.

Yet it's the briefest of seasons, and what time there is in summer is carried forward by wind, by Boreas, god of the north wind, who, it's said, can blow out of two or more cheeks at once.

June 23. A breeze stiffens. Gusts are clocked at forty-five, sixty, eighty-five miles per hour. Rainless thunderclouds crack above, shaking pine pollen down. *La bufera infernale*— that's what Dante calls winds that lashed at sinners in hell. I decide to go out in the infernal storm. "This is hell," a herder moving his sheep across the mountain says, grinning; then he clears his parched throat and rides away. Wind carries me back and forth, twisting, punching me down.

I'm alone here for much of the summer, these hot winds my only dancing partner. The sheep and their herder vanish over a ridge. I close my eyes, and the planet is auditory only: tree branches twist into tubas and saxes, are caught by large hands that press down valves, and everywhere on this ranch I hear feral music—ghostly tunes made not by animals gone wild but by grasses, sagebrush, and fence wire singing.

The next day, or the next. The wind stops and the temperature soars. I've given up my hunt for the origin of summer and instead take off my clothes and lie on the grass in front of the house, trying to find, in the noonday sun, heat's grace. Sweat rolls from my face. Summer feels like a form of stasis: the oscillations of subatomic particles seem to rock less, vigilance is lost, and the axial wobbling of Earth steadies . . . or does it? In my journal no words, only a drawing of a stick figure (me) grasping a huge straw, ever uncertain, wondering how so many opposing thoughts can be contained in one head. A Sung dynasty poet writes: "The city is full of flying pear flowers." I imagine a blizzard, the sky solid with blossoms, white noise, white heat.

June 30. A heavy plane lumbers upward and circles near the mountains. It's a World War II bomber carrying slurry, bound for distant fire. My own tiny twig fire is almost out. On it I'd cooked a dinner of elk steaks, half an onion, a green pepper. My bedroll laid out, I sleep on the ground until the wind wakes me. It's 10:30 P.M. Night closes down over gasping trees; the clipped laughter and a cappella chants of coyotes by the house beat the dry dome of the ground. I lie on my back. This treasure hunt for summer has been a farce, especially now, since I know how the season arrived: wind served it up on a silver platter, but a platter hurled like an Olympian's discus, metallic and hard—*la bufera infernale*. Then, at midnight, I see how wind is only an ocean held in by night's black hood.

A slurry bomber awakens me. It's the middle of July, and the wave of heat that swelled in June now arches over my head. Summer's heat is a koan, an answerless question. All I know is this: gravity rains bugs down from sources of light; botflies crawl out of dung; heat waves break over the roof of my mouth as if it were coral, its calcareous skeleton washed wet, then dry. Corals, being marine animals, shed eggs and sperm into the sea, and free-swimming larvae latch onto old colonies and secrete new skeletons; above the roof of my mouth I imagine brain coral. Ideas swim, fertilize, and reproduce. Skeletal forms called theca merge, and at the end of each deep channel of thought, the koan, the riddle, floats on its back heedlessly.

Persistent heat pushes the thermometer to 102 degrees, then 105 degrees, and the sky balloons, featureless. Behind smoke from forest fires the sun rises bloodied and sets bloodied, and the moon is a half-eaten peach midsky. The long summer twilights I'd longed for all winter are obscured. I turn on house lights at 5:00 P.M. and, scanning the sky, wonder if the moon is reflecting not sunlight but the light from fires.

Midsummer means cattle are on the range. Ducks on the lake are half grown but still can't fly, and the birds that pass through in their dash from South America to the north—terns, godwits, sora rails, phalaropes—are long gone. Smoke blues the sidehills of this valley. I think of my dead grandmother's hair tinted pink, turning blue at death. "Turn on the lights, turn on the lights," she kept saying when she was dying, and that's what I say to the sky now.

Fires in the Bighorn, Beartooth, and Absaroka mountains flare like sunspots, making hellish day out of night. "Gloom of hell, gloom of night uncomforted," Dante writes. Night consists of smoke. No human presence here. Then visitors come through: a retired rancher, a photographer, a child, a woman who danced in the New York City Ballet. I tell them there are ten-thousand-foot peaks directly behind the house, but they are skeptical. Rolling smoke has bulldozed all that. We work in the garden harvesting beans, then eat, drink, and dance, pirouetting on dead grass under a lidded sky, with no constellations to tell us in which direction to turn our lives.

After they leave, alone again, I sometimes sleep through the afternoon, stupefied by heat, and between wolf naps read more Dante. By chance I turn to the second circle of the *Inferno,* the realm of lust. One is warned to go warily because of fires burning on either side of the path where spirits are passing; voices extol the virtues of chastity. Chastity . . . lust . . . what are they, and why has the waxing and waning of passion been bent into strict measures by rules?

July 17.   Summer's rapid heartbeat competes with that of the hummingbird who just mistook my red shirt for a flower and bombarded my chest. Reds dominate. At noon even the water holes where deer, elk, and cattle drink have a ruby tint. In Japan I read about the volcanic crater in northern Honshu where a shallow pond—the Pond of Blood—is likened to the pool of dirty blood from which a sinner must drink. Summer is not about fruition but about conflagration—the pear flowers streaming through are really white ash. All day I lean toward what shimmers and dazzles: the hard, obsequious diamonds of light on our half-dry lake, begging for rain and, like me, begging to be put out.

A friend from my home state, California, calls to tell me his child has just been christened in a seventeenth-century mission. "He laughed," my friend says. "And just as the holy water was being wiped from his forehead, a dog came to the entrance of the church and barked."

I think about how water crosses the land in a blind-man's buff through thatches of grass; how its percolation into the ground is the kind of blessing that cannot be wiped away except by wind. I think of how a child's head is wetted by sanctified water and how the sign of the cross is made just above the natural cross of bones in the body—sternum, spine, and pelvis—and wonder why blessings, in Christian churches, are applied to foreheads and not hearts, why part of the human skull has a religious name: temple, as if the cranial cavity were some kind of shrine.

In an irrigation ditch I set a tarp dam and turn water down the field from four notches. The human body is like so much plant life—green in its wanderings, the way the penis has a mind of its own, and the nipple; the way ideas are pressed upward to the tip of the brain stalk, pushing out of the skull like an inflorescence; the way these things are cut down.

Summer's natural fecundity both generates and is at odds with my emotional state: there is no moment without longing. And if longing implies an absence or the riddle of emptiness, then what fills me and why? On these solitary summer nights I long for company, yet by day, hearing a truck heave up our steep dirt road—perhaps a Sunday driver—I hide. Will the heat waves blur me sufficiently? That's what I wonder as I run to the top of the hay meadow where two fence lines meet in a creek. I crouch in the shade of a willow until the truck leaves. Locusts line the branches, making sounds like rattlesnakes. In the dust bowl days, a rancher told me, locusts ate all the bark off fence posts and trees. I dangle my feet, shoes and all, in the creek. Tiny islands split water as if showing how separate truths—like separate, simultaneous loves—can be found in the same story.

It is the third week of July. I notice now my days are cut in half: mornings I contemplate repletion, afternoons I consider thirst. Today I go for a walk but turn back. No cobalt skies lure me on. During a drought, space shrinks, and only time, like a tongue swelling, grows between me and those I love. I'm unable to give words to flashing and darkening thoughts, or to swim the alternating current of revulsion and desire. There is no stir in the air. My legs are tiny straws trying to move the wide drink of air but failing. Yet even in this claustral, motionless heat there is an inward billowing. Heat waves carry me upward on their snake charmer backs, and for a moment I catch a wild scrawl of fragrance—not smoke but wild rose.

At dusk smoke looks like coastal fog, and the mountains are California's Channel Islands, which I could see from my childhood bed. Fog brings with it the smell of life—of the sea, of celery, flowers, garlic, and oranges growing. It stands for its opposite: possibility, not occlusion. Elk, shouldering mist, drift through pine forests; now bombers carrying fire retardant boom in the half-dark, and, sleepily, I mistake them for the sound of tectonic plates stirring.

July 30.   Tonight it's too hot to sleep in the house. Even the horse I saddle to ride into the mountains, where it will be cooler, is anxious to escape. He runs to me when I appear in the pasture with a bridle looped over my arm. There is no moonlight, but we know the way. Quickly the rasp of sagebrush gives way to the whir of pine, and the smoke smell mixes with wild geranium. Aspens tick in the breeze as if counting off the elevation: seven thousand eight hundred and one; eight thousand and eight . . . In the dark I enter a high, wide bowl and ride through the castanets of wild irises gone to seed: clickety-clack go the dry seed-heads as my horse's front legs hit them, but no fandangos are danced tonight.

July 31.   At the end of the day, I come to this: there's a sameness to the extravagances of every season, to the promiscuousness of pollinators, the abundance of seed produced, to the way we press ourselves on a hot night to what Robinson Jeffers calls "the careless white bone of things," to the way the ruthless second hand cuts down months like hay.

A middle-of-the-night thunderstorm awakens me. It brings no rain, but lightning's light pierces my eyelids, and for a moment the elusive shapes of summer—the hipbones and elbows of a mountain's body, or a lover's—jut up above the general haze, breaking welds that have bound desire to despair.

Igor Stravinsky said at the end of his life that he thought his blood had thickened into rubies. That's how August looks: a ruby sun descends through leaves and layers of smoke like an elevator falling through an abandoned building. What kind of edifice is this season of summer, that it looks empty when it is ripe, that crystallized blood is flushed like musical notes from the head?

On August fifth, it rained for three minutes, but it was like water dropping on a hot griddle. New fires have erupted and are given names: the Clover, Mist, Mink. Now a cool mistral fingers my horse's mane, and the shade a departing rain cloud makes grazes the green grass in front of me as I ride to find stray cattle.

Dante thought that shades were souls who had been freed from their bodies but still retained intelligence. I see shades and shadows everywhere. But what to make of them? When the sky clears, even the lake takes on the gray, as if inhaling smoke; cattails brandish brown torches that have burned; and in the west, cinnamon-colored smoke mushrooms upward like the spew of a dropped bomb. Tomorrow: Hiroshima Day.

August 6. The evening news brings it all back: from the hijacking of superior minds to work on the Manhattan Project, the first detonation at the Trinity site, viewed from bunkers ten and twenty miles away; to the loading of the bomb on the *Enola Gay,* a plane named for the pilot's mother; and on a quiet morning the dropping of the bomb on a sizable Japanese city through which the Ota River runs; then the permanent shadows cast on stone by heat, and the skin and hair that would not stay attached, and the dead horses floating in the river, and the black rain. . . .

Walking from the house, I remember the day Chernobyl blew, the two clouds of radiation that met over Wyoming and the rain that came as I was irrigating the fields; how sudden, darkening skies tarnished what is hopeful about vivid green.

Now summer's supine sky appears to be sealed when it is not. The myth of inviolability, the idea that no force could shred skin from our faces, implies a refusal to believe we can cause harm. At the end of this evening's news we were given updates on the holes in the ozone, as if now we were tossing bombs or bayonets upward, tearing the skin of the sky. I try to unwind one thread from these enormous catastrophes all the way back to my heart, to any human heart, to see if anywhere along the way an instinct for care exists. What shocks me so is the detachment with which we dispense destruction—not just bombs, but blows to the head of the earth, to populations of insects, plants, and animals, and to one another with senseless betrayal—and how the proposed solutions are always mechanistic, as if we could fabricate the health of the planet the way we make a new car.

August 7. I walk to the lake in the morning. My blue canoe is loose. Blue, the color of ozone, that poisonous, explosive gas made from one too many oxygen atoms. I watch the boat glide, smoothing out hard angles of light on water, recutting them, as if to say possibility still exists, if only we could direct our lives so that peace, which can be achieved only by peaceful means, could be embedded like garden seeds in our actions, ideas, and goals.

Days later I bumped my head on the top of the pump house door and surprised myself by sobbing. It wasn't the pain but the memory of having hit my head hard two summers ago, when the colt I was riding bucked so unexpectedly. I landed headfirst and came up in a daze. There were cuts on my mouth and neck; slivers of rock slid under my skin like shrapnel, and are with me still. The next day I had trouble seeing. Clots of blood, bunched like grapes, appeared behind my eyes, and when I was taken to the hospital, the doctor gleefully announced that I'd have to have holes drilled in my skull to relieve the pressure on my brain. To my look of horror he said only, "I really do hate horses."

Inside the CAT scan I experienced unearthly peace: the capsule white, the noise white, the body held motionless by straps. It was comforting. I fell asleep and dreamed I was blind but could see hills washed by lightning. The people in the dream were opalescent; only the animals had ruby red blood.

Dante writes in the *Inferno* that the damned were unable to see the present but could foretell the future. In Japan, among other places, physical blindness is thought to bring on a kind of inward vision. In the Ōu Mountains of northern Honshu, mediums called *itako*—blind women—are hired to perform divinations and to communicate with the dead.

At home, I lay on the couch. The brain in the process of mending feels like Jell-O being pressed through dry hands. Aside from the roaring in my ears, all senses and desires were deadened, and even with regained sight, my inward life was a blank, my outward one had no meaning. Friends came by. I looked normal enough, but how could I explain the bruised heat or the coolness of no desire? Now the blindness and deadness is not mine but the sky's.

August 12. Determined to transpierce this wall of smoke, I scan the sky with new resolve. Why has this smoke-flattened landscape become an inward torment? All I see is gray and cinnamon rolling into gray. Hope comes from a friend—a geophysicist—who calls on the phone. He has news: using seismological equipment, he has begun mapping out a topography of the earth's molten core by measuring the velocity of pressure waves. Below the earth's crust, down through the two-thousand-mile-thick mantle, the core has its own unique landscape, complete with mountains and hot oceans and a geological weather in which turbulent eddies of iron splinters rain down. "It's like seeing form come into being," he says. I try to do the same with smoke, to sense the ghosts and the landscapes it hides, the shape and weight of desire.

August 16. More fires erupt. A big hand is dropping matches all over the West. Like winged seeds, sparks are propelled into the sky, scratching and scarring its skin. Then the smoke goes and the sky bulges in Gothic arches of blue. To hell with rubies, I say. The sky is sapphire, hyacinth, robin's egg blue. My head feels light: smoke's vise has been removed.

Tonight, for the first time in thirty-nine nights, I can see stars. I lay my bedroll on the ground in front of the house and gather my dogs around. "There's Sirius," I say, pointing to the Dog Star, but quickly they fall asleep. The Milky Way rolls over me; it has turned the scroll of the sky from gray to blue to black and filled it with clouds of stars whose luminous galactic centers are fueled by streams of dust and gas fifteen light-years long. . . . My God, how I've missed this: the contrast of light and dark, time gone wild, star deaths, pulsars spinning out a whole day in one two-thousandth of a second as if spinning time into matter and matter into radio noises, into what one astronomer I know calls "crackling, night-chanting songs."

A meteor bursts over my head. It's not a shower but a strike, a high fly ball hit hard. August is the month of the Perseid meteor showers. Twenty-eight years ago I watched them from the deck of a broad-beamed gaff-rigged schooner. They looked like the orchids my mother grew in the house, though secretly I thought of the "falling stars" as eyes searching the sea, attracted by our boat's running lights.

Now I'm landlocked and drought-stricken in Wyoming, my husband gone for the summer, my longed-for solitude having spoiled to lethargy. Every thought feels like an accident; how remote I am, sitting on the edge of this one galaxy where planet Earth and its little sun do their whirling dervish to no one's astonishment or applause.

Even the sky's clarity, in which I've rejoiced tonight, is not what it seems: a thousand tons of galactic dust falls into the atmosphere every day, galactic debris of all kinds—chunks of comets snatched out of the Oort cloud, hurled toward Earth and heated to incandescence, with ionized tails so long and bright they cast shadows, *shades* bigger than any ghosts I know.

I think of Tanabata, celebrated this month in Japan when two stars, Altair and Vega, cross the "River of Heaven"—the Milky Way—and meet like the legendary lovers who are allowed only one night of love a year. Up and down the Kamo River young girls write the names of those they love on strips of rice paper and tie them to stalks of bamboo that are fastened to the eaves of the house. . . .

In the dark, in the wind, I scrape my ink block, apply brush to rice paper, and write names. . . .

. . .

August 18.   High up on the mountain slope I snooze, the stone tablets to the northwest shrugging their shoulders above my head. When I wake, I'm eyeball-to-eyeball with a thumb-sized fern curled under a rock. With no water since June 12, how has it survived?

From my nearly vertical perch I feel a sense of apocalyptic gaiety as I watch smoke from new fires billowing. For almost a hundred years, park and forest managers have enforced a policy of fire suppression, "to preserve natural beauty," because under "beauty" there is no slot for burned ground. Now nature has put her match to over a million acres of unnaturally preserved timber whose beauty has always eluded me. So thick, so monocultural, it is but another kind of screen: green, not gray.

By mistake a pilot drops slurry on the Wyoming town of Buffalo, and an arsonist reverses the mistake by setting fire to a Main Street store. El Niño gives way to La Niña, her cold waters humping warm streams northward, pushing the jet stream that brings rain too far into Canada to do us any good.

I call a friend at Yellowstone Park's headquarters. We talk dew points, moisture profiles, the fact that these fires are nature's way of burning excess fuel, and ponder for a moment the possibility of the entire West going up in flames as a result of spontaneous combustion.

At night I lie on my humble blanket, made in Mexico of twisted rags. Usually it's the moon that is the lantern in the sky, and I feel wind taking part of the waterfall and laying it softly on my face, shunting rushing-water noise into vertical waves as if a radio had been turned on. But tonight the whole sky is an unlit lamp, a hanging weight, a tide of heat waves ramming my abdomen and lungs.

It was another year but the same day when a spell of breathlessness overtook me. I met a man who had already "given his heart away." Our coming together was like being slugged in the gut, and the deep inhalations that began racking me were silent yelps of surprise and despair. For weeks after, I thought myself pregnant when I wasn't, as if the body were free to follow its own loving course. I imagined multiple fathers for one insubstantial child, or else one father—him—for the many children I hadn't had, all conceived before we met.

Conjoined, oblivious, love turned into hyperventilation—Boreas blowing out of every cheek until he fainted and my breathlessness congealing into anguished sobs. "Impossible," we said to each other, as though saying another kind of vow. The winds that blew us, first in the direction of oneness, reversed, quickly erasing the marks of love with exhaustion's hopeless velocity.

Morning, the nineteenth.   By seven, it's ninety degrees. In a monastery where I once stayed, a monk warned me about asking too many "historical" questions. But I say what Pedro, a sheepherder, says: *"La vida es muy histórica"*—life *is* history, full of stories. The monk quoted from the Chinese: "Too many steps have been taken to the root and the source. Better to have been blind and deaf from the beginning . . . dwelling in one's true abode, unconcerned."

Walking home from the waterfall, I argue with myself. Isn't one's true abode any wild place, any fire storm or night of discontent, and isn't a book of essays truly a book of questions? As I walk, smoke is supplanted by brightening clouds; the moon—and all desire for what is not—rides out of the sky.

August 20.   Some 160,000 acres burn today. (Later it would be dubbed Black Saturday.) This added to the 273,000 acres already burned over within park boundaries. But when they say burn, they mean simply that fire has passed through, burning some spots hot and only blowing sparks through others.

Visibility has dropped to zero. In town, people drive with their lights on. No longer a thing of the sky, smoke rolls along the ground. There is no sun. Fire rearranges light the way light reorders landscape. I stand in the middle of a field and try to see . . . anything. The apple tree, full of fruit, shakes. The air is red, and the white falling everywhere is not snow but ash, as if decay preceded fruition, or night, day. Something hits my face. I hold out my hands: the burnt casings of pine cones, charred needles, and burnt twigs from a hundred miles away rain down.

My neighbor Joe and I recompose weather bulletins. When the radio says "Scattered clouds," we change it to "Continued hot, scattered forests, heavy at times."

September 3.   Fire moves: elk and bison run before the wind. Fire jumps canyons and grizzly bears' den sites and flies over shaky-legged oxbows where swans swim un-alarmed. Flame builds to massive walls; it gathers whole forests with double-jointed arms, laying down life as ash, or else takes only what is green, leaving behind ideas about what a national park should be, and even those are charred.

Friends—one of them a colonel who taught English at West Point—arrive to take a pack trip with me. "What war am I in?" Pat, a veteran of Korea and Vietnam, asks as he gets off the plane. The Tetons, a quarter of a mile away, cannot be seen.

The Jackson Hole airport resembles a war zone. Army helicopters—twin-rotor Chinooks and the smaller Hueys—are lined up at the far edge of the field. They're being used for troop transport, cargo, medevacking, and water drops—a thousand pounds at a time—but today they're grounded by smoke.

A makeshift, boxlike lookout has been constructed out of blue tarps and two-by-fours on top of the terminal roof and is manned by someone with binoculars, who reports the movement of military aircraft to the controllers keeping track of commercial planes. A battered white station wagon pulls up. The sign taped to its door reads: FIRE SHUTTLE. The terminal is packed. It's a crowd of uniformed men and women from the Army, the Forest Service, the Bureau of Land Management, the Game and Fish Department, plus exhausted and fresh-faced firefighters including Apaches and Sho-Raps (Shoshone and Arapaho), the Mendocino Hotshot Crew, firefighters from Alaska and Hawaii, all mixed in with bewildered tourists, who have just flown in from places with bluer skies.

I'm handed a Fire Status Update Sheet for 9/3/88. It tells me that 877,805 acres have burned; total personnel fighting the fire is 9,069, and the cost so far is $63,183,400.

Before I even get to the mountains I ask this question: Why are we spending roughly three million dollars a day on a fire that everyone but the politicians have agreed cannot be put out by any human effort? Is it because we are so vain, so enamored with technology, that we can't admit something is bigger than we can comprehend? The fire-fighters I talk with agree: "We dig hand lines—bulldozers aren't allowed, they're not 'natural'—and then hike five miles out, knowing that in an hour or two the fire will jump our line. So what are we doing here?"

Another firefighter said with a wry smile: "You want to know what the human role is here? To do what the animals do—run the hell out of the fire's way."

After gathering at the trailhead, we ride north from Brooks Lake, following Cub Creek into the wilderness on a route not far from the eastern perimeter of the Mink Creek fire. A water ouzel—John Muir's favorite bird—flies low and fast upcreek as if to lead our long packstring away from the conflagration. Six miles in, we make a quick overnight camp. Because no open fires are allowed, we cook on a fold-up sheet-metal stove and watch the pencil-point flame extend beyond the stovepipe: fire pointing to fire.

The next day. We ride up finger meadows walled three thousand feet high with conglomerate rock—volcanic debris spewed from huge vents and taken away in rivers of coarse-grained hot rock that were later widened by water. Now we're in and out of shade, through patches of trees. A marsh hawk eyes us. Elk thistles are dead stumps; the grasses are sun-cured. Only fireweed catches my eye: where its red leaves turn back in dryness, a delicate pale pink shows. Above me are patches of timber whose deadfall looks like white legs hanging down; vertical clefts in rock are waterfalls gone dry, and overhead, smoke streams blow endlessly. . . .

At the confluence of two creeks, ten miles from the edge of the Mink Creek fire, I finally see flame: a salmon band at the western horizon, that's all. Then smoke, my constant summer companion, unfurls itself at my feet, spreading across the valley floor, holding me in its troubled lens.

That the fires are a benefit to plant life is indisputable. Two hundred years of deadfall is being cleaned up, meadows are cleared and widened, the monoculture of lodgepole pine is broken apart so that other species, like whitebark pine (whose nuts are an important food source for grizzlies), can grow. The grass will come back with vigor, as will berries and shrubs, though the regrowth of trees in this arid western state will take years. With plant diversity comes animal diversity—that's the ladder on which flora and fauna have coevolved.

Native Americans used the Yellowstone area for ten thousand years (maybe more), but until 1972 national park policy favored fire suppression instead of allowing natural fires to burn in order to clear timber, improve vegetation, and flush out game for hunting, as the Indians had. With our racism intact and our obsession with what is new, it was thought that nothing useful could be learned from their "old ways." Native Americans—the Tukarika (Sheep-eaters) among others—had been expelled from the park in 1882, ten years after its inception, because it was thought their presence might deter tourists. If burning—Indian style—had been allowed all along, we might not be running from what is fast becoming a single, holocaustal fire now and hiring Native American hotshot fire crews to put it out.

Nature and culture. How confused we've become.

Being human, we're part of nature as well as being culture makers. Yet the messy, living, vital interconnections elude us still.

September 6. We've moved our camp to higher ground, and today I walk atop the Buffalo Plateau, a treeless landscape strewn with rock. I lie on my back, letting the stones warm me. Ash falls on my face like powdered sugar, my feet pointed west toward flames. Fires above; fires below—Yellowstone burning doubly. The ground under me is the child of fire: massive volcanic flows of welded tufts, breccia, rhyolite, basalt, obsidian; tubes of fire cutting through the earth's crust like an acetylene torch, hot magma pressing upward through faults, molten rock heating groundwater to boiling, erupting, dancing on the shores of Yellowstone Lake, which rests in the arms of a caldera.

Sitting cross-legged on my bed of rocks, I open my mouth: an ash alights on my tongue. I swallow. . . . *This is the body of . . .* What have I eaten? A piece of tree, of fire; a piece of this island universe, or just ash, that solid residue of combustion? I no longer contemplate the sky; it kneels down on me: smoke works the landscape into invisibility.

All summer I've tried to escape darkness, the smoke-induced gloom, but in doing so I've only blocked out light. I've endowed smoke with solidity. It has clothed me, it's been my faulty lens. But form does not imply a restriction, a limitation. Like the geophysicists who are trying to "see" into the core of the earth, I must learn to see the open dimension of form—to move through, not against, the obstacles I set up for myself.

Walking back to camp, I realize I'm lost. Smoke has swallowed all landmarks. But why must I see to know something? I let my feet take me. At sunset the gray flannel sky turns red. It's a thick broth made of rubies and plasma—comet tails, plant seeds, human and animal blood rising up from fire. I think, as I walk, of the way I put up smoke screens, distancing myself so subtly from what is real, intrinsic, primordial, the ways in which I keep ego's circulation smooth, adding smoke to smoke.

When the red goes out of the sky, I know the sun is down. A long, traversing trail leads me to camp. There will be no campfire to comfort me. Instead I crawl into my bedroll. Night is the backdrop against which desire for what is not has been thrown like a dart. Against night, against all progress toward morning, the sparks that drop from my forehead are not the eloquent words I'd once hoped for but only pieces of thought—what is left over after grammar and syntax are burned away.

September 9. Woke feeling warm even though there is ice on the creek. For two days we've been checking grizzly tracks near camp. I can see the deep gouge the grizzly's heel made, the lines on the palm of his "hand," and the arc of claws. "When I'm following tracks," Jack says, "I feel I'm only seeing punctuation and nouns, not the actual thing, the verbs, the animals who made them." Farther up the mountain we cross a moonscape—a dry lakebed of cracked earth and rocks shaped like the fish who once swam here. From the top we see fire. It is closing in on us, and we may have to run. During the night we take turns checking the flames. Saffron and pink light balloons inside gray smoke clouds;

golden trout jumping in the lake below look like pieces of fire.

Later, back at camp, a wind that smells like snow carries the stars into place. From my sleeping bag I watch the Milky Way roll west and think of lines from Tu Fu:

Borne headlong
Toward the long shadows of sunset
By headstrong, stubborn moments,
Life whirls past like drunken wildfire.

September 10. I wake to rain. *Rain,* for God's sake. Rain that turns to snow and keeps coming, quietly extinguishing the summer-long wildfires. Smoke begins to clear out; smoke and steam rise together, entwined.

Newly bathed, the planet gives off vapors. Down from the high country, fording rivers, I ride through dripping trees for eight hours. Trees are midpoint between seed and ash, always rising, always fighting for sunlight. Yet the literal shade they make with their dense canopies darkens the ground. I try to imagine the places where fire has been, where trees are no more, how landscape is bathed by rain and will soon bask in sunlight, and wonder if barren ground is the end of fruition, if it is, to quote Wallace Stevens, the "fertile thing that can attain no more."

Late September. La bufera infernale blows less frequently now, and for the time being, Boreas's cheeks are flat. Stillness gives the illusion of longevity, even immortality, yet I clock the days as if clocking the length of human life.

The ground is rain-soaked, but days are bright: the planet is a burning ember that will not go out.

In October my husband and I ride to hunting camp. At ten thousand feet, his white-wall tents are set in pines and backed up to a ledge of pink granite that topples into a gorge. Lanterns hang from the ridgepole of the cooktent. They swing and hiss in the wind, but when I blow them out, the aurora relights my bed. Bright spires stab, pulse, and plume diagonally, pinning us to the ground, then explode like scarves being dropped. I think of Dante clutching his beloved Beatrice's hand as they move from the sphere of fire to Paradise. Folds of blue and green are taken over by reds that deepen in hue: electrons colliding with atoms and molecules.

The Labrador Eskimos thought the aurora borealis was caused by fire, that the lights were torches held by spirits taking the souls of the newly dead to the afterworld. In the morning Press shoots a dry doe so we'll have meat for the winter. It's not a happy moment watching an animal go down.

"Forgive us your suffering," I say, kneeling by the deer, and wonder what a soul looks like as it lifts out of flesh. As I watch the knife cut through the brisket, then down the length of the animal through the udder, where the milk would have been if she'd had a fawn, the euphemism that calls this act "dressing out an animal" seems obscene. It's more like an undressing in the extreme: steaming guts in cool air, all those intestines . . . then the legs cut off at the knee, and finally the head.

In Japan's northern Honshu, people think the dead go to one mountain, and in some provinces relatives climb the roofs of their houses to call the soul back. I arrange the dead doe's severed legs, then face the detached head, pointing east. The sun is going down in the west, where the fires once burned and the first snow of the season has already been laid on the ground, yet her flesh is warm and her thick ear soft. I lean down. In death, her eyes have turned aquamarine.

We ride out at dark—three hours. In a meadow after a steep drop down a trail, the leggy white trunks of aspen look like spires of light—spirit streamers or torches carrying the wild soul of a dead deer and lifting it to a place over the roof of my head onto which my voice climbs, calling. . . .

ISLAND

I come to this island because I have to. Only geography can frame my mind, only water can make my body stop. I come, not for solitude—I've had enough of that in my life—but for the discipline an island imposes, the way it shapes the movement of thoughts.

Humpbacked, willow-fringed, the island is the size of a boat, roughly eighty-five feet by twenty, and lies on the eastern edge of a small man-made lake on our Wyoming ranch. I call this island Alcatraz because I once mistook a rare whooping crane that had alighted in the lower field for a pelican, and that's what the Spanish *alcatraz* means: pelican. But the name was also a joking reference to the prison island I threatened to send my saddle horse to if he was bad, though in fact *my* Alcatraz was his favorite spot on the ranch to graze.

Now Blue is dead, and I have the island to myself. Some days, Rusty, my thirteen-year-old working dog, accompanies me, sitting when I sit, taking in the view. But a view is something our minds make of a place, it is a physical frame around natural fact, a two-way transmission during which the land shapes our eyes and our eyes cut the land into "scapes."

I sit to sweep the mind. Leaves, which I think of as a tree's discontinuous skin, keep falling as if mocking my attempts to see past my own skin, past the rueful, cantankerous, despairing, laughing racket in my head.

At water's edge the tiny leaves of wild rose are burned a rusty magenta, and their fruit, still unpicked by birds, hangs like drops of blood. Sun on water is bright: a blind that keeps my mind from wandering. The ripples are grooves the needle of memory makes, then they are the lines between which music is written—quintets of bird song and wind. The dam bank is a long thigh holding all restlessness in.

To think of an island as a singular speck or a monument to human isolation is missing the point. Islands beget islands: a terrestrial island is surrounded by an island of water, which is surrounded by an island of air, all of which makes up our island universe. That's how the mind works too: one idea unspools into a million concentric thoughts. To sit on an island, then, is not a way of disconnecting ourselves but, rather, a way we can understand relatedness.

Today the island is covered with duck down. It is the

time of year when mallards molt. The old, battered flight feathers from the previous spring are discarded, and during the two or three weeks it takes for the new ones to grow in, they can't fly. The males, having lost their iridescent plumage, perform military maneuvers on the water, all dressed in the same drab uniform.

Another definition of the word "island" is "the small isolated space between the lines in a fingerprint," between the lines that mark each of us as being unique. An island, then, can stand for all that occurs between thoughts, feathers, fingerprints, and lives, although, like the space between tree branches and leaves, for example, it is part of how a thing is shaped. Without that space, trees, rooms, ducks, and imaginations would collapse.

Now it's January, and winter is a new moon that skates the sky, pushing mercury down into its tube. In the middle of the night the temperature drops to thirty-two below zero. Finally, the cold breaks, and soon the groundhog will cast a shadow, but not here. Solitude has become a reflex: when I look at the lake no reflection appears. Yet there are unseen presences. Looking up after drinking from a creek, I see who I'm not: far up on a rock ledge, a mountain lion, paws crossed, has been watching me.

Later in the month, snow on the lake melts off, and the dendritic cracks in ice reappear. The lake is a gray brain I pose questions to. Somewhere in my reading I come on a reference to the island of Reil. It is the name given to the central lobe of the cerebral hemisphere deep in the lateral tissue, the place where the division between left and right brain occurs, between what the neurobiologist Francisco Varela calls "the net and the tree."

To separate out thoughts into islands is the peculiar

way we humans have of knowing something, of locating ourselves on the planet and in society. We string events into temporal arrangements like pearls or archipelagos. While waiting out winter, I listen to my mind switch from logic to intuition, from tree to net, the one unbalancing the other so no dictatorships can stay.

Now snow collapses into itself under bright sun with a sound like muffled laughter. My young friend Will, aged nineteen, who is suffering from brain cancer, believes in the laughing cure, the mango cure, the Molokai cure, the lobster cure—eating what pleases him when he can eat, traveling to island paradises when he can walk, astonished by the reversal of expectation that a life must last a certain number of years.

In the evening I watch six ravens make a playground of the sky. They fly in pairs, the ones on the left, for no reason, doing rolls like stunt pilots. Under them, the self-regulating planet moves and the landscape changes—fall to winter, winter to spring, suffering its own terminal diseases in such a way that I know nothing is unseasonal, no death is unnatural, nothing escapes a raven's acrobatic glee.

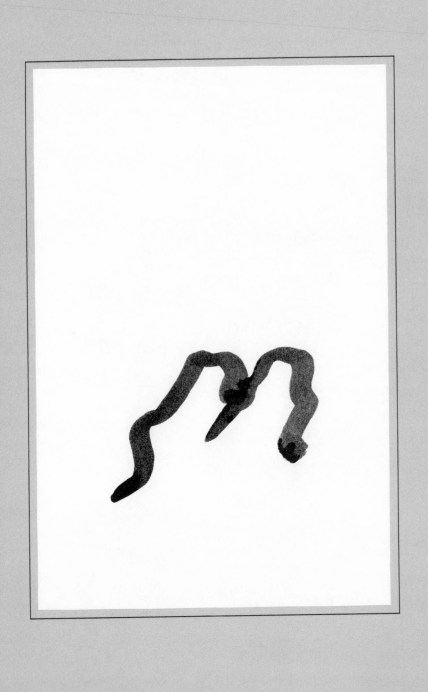

THIS AUTUMN MORNING

We are both in dreams, appearing in dream forms. I add
words spoken in sleep: Turn this way; I'm lonely too this
autumn evening.

MATSUO BASHŌ

*W*hen did all this happen, this rain and snow
bending green branches, this turning of light
to shadow in my throat, these bird notes going flat, and how
did these sawtooth willow leaves unscrew themselves from
the twig, and the hard, bright paths trampled into the hills
loosen themselves to mud? When did the wind begin churn-
ing inside trees, and why did the sixty-million-year-old
mountains start looking like two uplifted hands holding and
releasing the gargled, whistling, echoing grunts of bull elk,
and when did the loose fires inside me begin *not* to burn?

Wasn't it only last week, in August, that I saw the

stained glass of a monarch butterfly clasping a purple thistle flower, then rising as if a whole cathedral had taken flight? And didn't Dante and Beatrice, whose journey I have been tracing, finally rise from fire to Paradise?

Now what looks like smoke is only mare's tails—clouds streaming—and as the season changes, my young dog and I wonder if raindrops might not be shattered lightning.

It's September. Light is on the wane. There is no fresh green breast of earth to embrace. None of that. Just to breathe is a kind of violence against death. To long for love, to have experienced passion's deep pleasure, even once, is to understand the mercilessness of having a human body whose memory rides desire's back unanchored from season to season.

Last night while driving to town I hit a deer. She jumped into my path from behind bushes so close I could not stop. A piece of red flesh flew up and hit the windshield. I watched as she ran off limping. There was nothing I could do. Much later, on the way home, I looked for her again. I could see where a deer had bedded down beside a tree, but there was no sign of a wounded animal, so I continued on.

Halfway up our mountain road a falling star burned a red line across the sky—a meteorite, a pristine piece of galactic debris that came into existence billions of years before our solar system was made. The tail stretched out gold and slid. I stopped the truck. I was at the exact place where, years ago, I declared love to a friend, who grabbed his heart as if in pain, then said laconically, "What do you mean?"

Tonight on the same road in a different year I see only the zigzagging of foxes, whose red tails are long floats that give their small bodies buoyancy. No friends meet me to view the stars. The nights have turned cold. The crickets' summer mating songs have hardened into drumbeats, and dark rays of light pole out from under clouds as if steadying the flapping tent of the sky.

Even when the air is still I keep hearing a breeze, the way it shinnies up the bones of things, up the bark of trees. A hard frost pales the hayfields. Tucked into the flickering universe of a cottonwood tree, yellow leaves shaped like gloved hands reach across the green umbrella for autumn.

It's said that after fruition nothing will suffice, there is no more, but who can know the answer? I've decided to begin at the end when the earth is black and barren. I want to see how death is mixed in, how the final plurals are taken back to single things—if they are; how and where life stirs out of ash.

On May 5, the first day the roads opened, my husband and I drove to Yellowstone Park. Twenty miles before the east entrance, we were greeted by buffalo: four mother cows, one yearling, and a newly born calf. At Sylvan Pass a young couple were skiing down a precipitous snow-covered land-slide, then trudging up the nearly vertical slope carrying their skis. Just before we reached Yellowstone Lake, a pair of blue grouse, in the midst of a courting display, could not be moved from the center of the road. Neck and tail feathers plumed and fanned out; we waited. The lake was all ice. Far out, a logjam—upended, splintered, frozen in place— was the eye's only resting place in all that white.

At the next bend we came on a primordial scene: north of Mary's Bay, wide, ice-covered meadows were full of dead buffalo, and searching for grass in among the carcasses were the barely live bison who had survived a rigorous winter, so thin they looked like cardboard cutouts, a deep hollow between their withers and ribs.

We drove on. More dead bison, and dead elk. The Park biologists were saying that roughly twenty-eight percent of both herds had been winter-killed this year, not only because the fires diminished their forage but also because the drought had brought us five years of mild winters, thus allowing old and sick animals to survive.

Between Madison Junction and the Firehole River we stood in the charred ruins of a lodgepole pine forest. The hollow trunks of burned-out trees looked as if they had been picked up and dropped, coming to rest at every possible angle. The ground was black. Where the fire had burned underground, smoldering root systems upended trees; ponds and bogs that had supported waterfowl were now waterless depressions. Way back in the trees, a geyser hissed, its plume of white steam a ghost of the great fire's hundred-mile-long streamer of smoke.

Later we returned to the lake and sat on the end of a long spit of land that angles out into water. From there it's difficult to tell there was a fire. Lodgepole pines fringe the shore. A cloud that had moved off Mount Sheridan rolled toward us, its front edge buffeted by wind. In ancient Greece it was said that Boreas, god of the north wind, became jealous of his lover, Pitys, who had been flirting with Pan, and threw her against a rocky ledge. At that moment she turned into a pine tree. The amber drops of sap at the breaks of limbs are her tears.

Pines are ancient trees, having appeared 170 million years ago. The Buriat people in eastern Siberia consider groves of trees sacred and always ride through them in silence, while in Japan, pines stand for loyalty and longevity.

As I sat, the cloud took me midthought, slamming into the fringe of pines, shattering, becoming white needles.

That was May, and now it's September, and already frost is breaking down the green in leaves, then clotting like blood as tannin, anthocyanin, carotene, and xanthophyll. If pines represent continuance, then cottonwood leaves show me how the illusion of time punctuates space, how we fill those dusty, gaseous voids with escapades of life and death, dropping the tiny spans of human days into them.

This morning I found a yearling heifer, bred by a fence-jumping bull out of season, trying to calve. I saw her high up on a sage-covered slope, lying down, flicking her tail, and thought she must have colic. But I was wrong. The calf's front feet and head had already pushed out, who knows how many hours before, and it was dead.

I walked her down the mountain to the calving shed, where a friend, Ben, and I winched the dead calf out. We doctored the heifer for uterine infection, and I made a bed of straw, brought fresh creekwater and hay. The heifer ate and rested. By evening she had revived, but by the next morning she seemed to have pneumonia. Twenty cc's of penicillin later, she worsened. The antibiotics didn't kick in.

That night she lay down, emitting grunts and high-pitched squeals. The vet came at midnight. We considered every possibility—infection, pneumonia, poisoning—what else could it be? Another day, and her condition worsened. Not any one symptom but a steady decline. I emptied more medicine into her, knowing it was doing no good, but my conscience forbade me to do less. The vet came again and

left. He suggested it might be "hardware disease"—a euphemism for an ingested piece of metal, a nail or barbed
wire, cutting into her throat or stomach or heart. I put a
magnet down her throat. Strange as it seems, it sometimes
picks up the metal, taking it all the way through the digestive
tract. No response. I sat with her. I played music—Merle
Haggard and Mozart—wondering if my presence consoled
or irritated her. This was not a cow we had raised, and she
seemed unsure of me. Could a calf-puller, a shot-giver, *not*
mean harm?

That afternoon a phone call came telling me my dear
friend and mentor in all cowboying skills—"Mike"—had
suffered a heart attack. I drove hellbent to the hospital—
something told me there wasn't much time, but when I
entered the room, she sat up, elegant as ever, and we em-
barked on our usual conversation about horses, dogs, cattle,
and men. Despite a night of ferocious pain she looked beautiful. After an hour I reluctantly left to let her rest and went
home.

There I found the cow had not eaten or taken any
water. Her breathing was worse. I lay on the straw beside
her and slept. Before coming to the barn I had smelled
something acrid—the old, familiar smell of death, although
she was still alive. Yet the sounds she made now had changed
from grunting to a low moan, the kind of sound one makes
when giving in to something. She was dead by nightfall. In
the morning a second phone call came. My friend "Mike"
had "gone over the ridge."

Today yellow is combed all through the trees, and the heart-
shaped cottonwood leaves spin downward to nothingness. I

know how death is made—not why, but where in the body it begins, its lurking presence before the fact, its strangled music as if the neck of a violin were being choked; I know how breathing begins to catch on each rib, how the look of the eye flattens, gives up its depth, no longer sees past itself; I know how easily existence is squandered, how noiselessly love is dropped to the ground.

"You have to mix death into everything," a painter once told me. "Then you have to mix life into that," he said as his cigarette ashes dropped onto the palette. "If they are not there, I try to mix them in. Otherwise the painting won't be human." I was a child, and his words made me wince because it was my portrait he was painting. I wanted to be a painter at the time—I was twelve, and as far as I knew, death was something in a paint tube, to be squeezed out at will when you wanted to put in meaning.

Days later I walked to the graveyard. On a ranch, death is as much a constant as birth. The heifer was there with her calf, legs stretched out straight, belly bloated . . . but the white droppings of ravens—who were making a meal of her—cascaded down her rib cage like a waterfall.

I wandered through the scattered bones of other animals who have died. Two carcasses were still intact: Blue's and Lawyer's, saddle horses who put in many good years. Manes, tails, hair gone, their skin has hardened to rawhide, dried to a tautness, peeling back just slightly from ribs, noses, and hooves, revealing a hollow interior as if letting me see that the souls are really gone.

After fruition, after death, after black ash, perhaps there is something more, even if it is only the droppings of a scavenger, or bones pointing every which way as if to say,

"Touch here, touch here," and the velocity of the abyss when a loved one goes his way, and the way wind stirs hard over fresh graves, and the emptying out of souls into rooms and the mischief they get into, flipping switches, opening windows, knocking candles out of silver holders, and, after, shimmering on water like leaked gas ready to explode.

Mid-September. Afternoons I paddle my blue canoe across our nine-acre lake, letting water take me where it will. The canoe was a gift: eight dollars at the local thrift store.

As I drift aimlessly, ducks move out from the reeds, all mallards. Adaptable, omnivorous, and hardy, they nest here every year on the two tiny islands in the lake. After communal courtship and mating, the extra male ducks are chased away, but this year one stayed behind. Perhaps he fathered a clutch on the sly or was too young to know where else to go. When the ducklings hatched and began swimming, he often tagged along, keeping them loosely together until the official father sent him away. Then he'd swim the whole circumference of the lake alone, too bewildered and dignified to show defeat.

A green net of aquatic weeds knots the water, holding and releasing me as if I were weightless, as if I were loose change. Raised on the Pacific, I can row a boat, but I hardly know how to paddle. The water is either ink or a clear, bloodless liquid, and the black water snakes that writhe as I guide the canoe are trying to write words.

Evening. In Kyoto I was once taken to a moon-viewing room atop an ancient house on temple grounds. The room was square, and the windows on four sides were rice-paper cutouts framed by bamboo, rounds split down the center, allowing the viewer to re-create the moon's phase. To view the moon, one had to look through the moon of the window.

Tonight the lake is a mirror. The moon swims across. Every now and then I slide my paddle into its face. Last week I saw the moon rise twice in one night: once, heavy and orange—a harvest moon—heaving over the valley, and later, in the mountains, it was rising small, tight, and bright. Back in August the moon went blind. One night I sat outside with a bottle of wine and watched a shade pull across its difficult, cratered solitude. Thumbing through a book of late Tang poets, I came on an account of an eclipse: "But this night, the fifteenth of the eighth month, was not like other nights; for now we saw a strange thing: the rim was as though a strong man hacked off pieces with an ax," and "Darkness smeared the whole sky like soot, and then it seemed for thousands of ages the sky would never open."

Now with September almost gone, a half-moon slants down light and shadows move desolation all over the place. At dawn a flicker knocks. The hollow sound of his labor makes leaves drop in yellow skirts around the trunks of trees. Water bends daylight. Thoughts shift like whitecaps, wild and bitter. My gut is a harp. Its strings get plucked in advance of any two-way communication by people I love, so that I know when attentions wane or bloom, when someone dear goes from me. From the battered book of late T'ang poets I read this by Meng Chiao: "The danger of the road is not in the distance; ten yards is far enough to break a wheel. The peril of love is not in loving too often. A single evening can leave its wound in the soul."

Tonight thin spines of boreal light pin down thoughts as if skewered on the ends of thrown quills. I'm trying to understand how an empty tube behind a flower swells to fruit, how leaves twisting from trees are pieces of last year's fire spoiling to humus. Now trees are orange globes, their brightness billowing into cumulus clouds. As the sun rises, the barometer drops. Wind swings around, blasting me from the east, and every tin roof on the ranch shudders to a new tune.

Stripped of leaves, stripped of love, I run my hands over my single wound and remember how one man was like a light going up inside me, not flesh. Wind comes like horn blasts: the whole mountain range is gathered in one breath. Leaves keep coming off trees as if circulating through a fountain; steep groves of aspens glow.

I search for the possible in the impossible. Nothing. Then I try for the opposite, but the yellow leaves in trees— shaped like mouths—just laugh. Tell me, how can I shut out the longing to comprehend?

Wind slices pondswells, laying them sharp and flat. I paddle and paddle. Rain fires into the water all around me, denting the mirror. The pond goes colorless. Where the warm spring feeds in, a narrow lane has been cut through aquatic flowers to the deep end. I slide my canoe into the channel. Tendrils of duckweed wave green arms. Are they saying hello or good-bye?

Willows, clouds, and mountains lie in the lake's mirror, although they look as if they're standing. I dip my paddle and slide over great folds of time, through lapping depositions of memory, over Precambrian rock, then move inward, up a narrow gorge where a hidden waterfall gleams. After fruition, after death, water mirrors water.

The canoe slides to shore, and I get out. A cloud tears,

letting sun through, then closes again. I get down on my hands and knees and touch my tongue to water: the lake divides. Its body is chasm after chasm. Like water, I have no skin, only surface tension. How exposed I feel. Where a duck tips down to feed, one small ripple causes random turbidity, ceaseless chaos, and the lake won't stop breaking. *I can punch my finger through anything. . . .*

Much later, in the night, in the dark, I shine a flashlight down: my single wound is a bright scar that gives off hooked light like a new moon.

I try to cut things out of my heart, but the pack rat who has invaded my study won't let me. He has made himself the curator of my effects, my despair, my questioning, my memory. Every day a new show is installed. As if courting, he brings me bouquets of purple aster and sage gone to seed, cottonwood twigs whose leaves are the color of pumpkins. His scat is scattered like black rain: books, photographs, manuscripts are covered. The small offerings I set out years ago when I began using this room—a fistful of magpie feathers and the orange husks of two tangerines—have been gnawed into. Only the carved stone figure of a monk my mother gave me during tumultuous teenage years stands solid. The top of the narrow French desk where I write is strewn with cactus paddles—all lined up end to end—as if to remind me of how prickly the practice of vandalizing one's consciousness can be, how what seems inexpressible is like a thorn torn off under the skin.

The pack rat keeps me honest, and this is how: He reminds me that I've left something out. The summer after the fire, I returned to Yellowstone Park. I wanted to begin

again in barrenness, I wanted to understand ash. This time
the carcasses were gone—some eaten by bears, coyotes, eagles, and ravens; others taken away by the Park. Those
charnel grounds where only a green haze of vegetation
showed had become tall stands of grass. And the bison—
those who survived—were fat.

In a grassland at the northern end of the Park I stood
in fairy rings of ash where sagebrush had burned hot, and
saw how mauve-colored lupine seeds had been thrown by
twisted pods into those bare spots. At the edges were thumb-
nail-sized sage seedlings. Under a stand of charred Douglas
firs was a carpet of purple asters and knee-high pine grass,
in bloom for the first time in two hundred years—its inflorescence stimulated by fire. I saw a low-lying wild geranium
that appears only after a fire, then goes into dormancy again,
exhibiting a kind of patience I know nothing of. In another
blackened stand of trees it was possible to follow the exact
course of the burn by stepping only where pine grass was
in flower: ground fire had moved like rivulets of water. In
places where the fire burned hottest there was no grass,
because the organic matter in the soil had burned away, but
there were hundreds of lodgepole pine seedlings; the black
hills were covered with pink fireweed.

Just when all is black ash, something new happens.
Ash, of course, is a natural fertilizer, and now it's thought
to have a water-holding capacity: black ground is self-
irrigating in a self-regulating universe. How quickly "barrenness becomes a thousand things and so exists no more."

Now it's October. On the pond again, I hear water clank
against the patched hull. It is my favorite music, like that

made by halyards against aluminum masts. It is the music emptiness would compose if emptiness could change into something. The seat of my pants is wet because the broken seat in the canoe is a sponge holding last week's rainwater. All around me sun-parched meadows are green again.

In the evening the face of the mountain looks like a ruined city. Branches stripped bare of leaves are skeletons hung from a gray sky, and next to them are tall buildings of trees still on fire. Bands and bars of color are like layers of thought, moving the way stream water does, bending at point bars, eroding cutbanks. I lay my paddle down, letting the canoe drift. I can't help wondering how many ways water shapes the body, how the body shapes desire, how desire moves water, how water stirs color, how thought rises from land, how wind polishes thought, how spirit shapes matter, how a stream that carves through rock is shaped by rock.

Now the lake is flat, but the boat's wake—such as it is—pushes water into a confusion of changing patterns, new creations: black ink shifting to silver, and tiny riptides breaking forward-moving swells.

I glide across rolling clouds and ponder what my astronomer friend told me: that in those mysterious moments before the Big Bang there was no beginning, no tuning up of the orchestra, only a featureless simplicity, a stretch of emptiness more vast than a hundred billion Wyoming skies. By chance this quantum vacuum blipped as if a bar towel had been snapped, and resulted in a cosmic plasma that fluctuated into and out of existence, finally moving in the direction of life.

"But where did the bar towel come from?" I asked my

friend. He laughed. No answer. Somehow life proceeded from artlessness and instability, burping into a wild diversity that follows no linear rules. Yet in all this indeterminacy, life keeps opting for life. Galactic clouds show a propensity to become organic, not inorganic, matter; carbon-rich meteorites have seeded our earthly oasis with rich carbon-based compounds; sea vents let out juvenile water warm enough to generate growth, and sea meadows brew up a marine plasma—matter that is a thousandth of a millimeter wide—and thus give rise to all plant life and the fish, insects, and animals with which it coevolved.

I dip my paddle. The canoe pivots around. Somewhere out there in the cosmos, shock waves collapsed gas and dust into a swirl of matter made of star grains so delicate as to resemble smoke, slowly aggregating, gradually sweeping up and colliding with enough material to become a planet like ours.

Dusk. A bubble of cloud rises over the mountain. It looks like the moon, then a rock tooth pierces it, and wind burnishes the pieces into soft puffs of mist. Forms dissolve into other forms: a horsehead becomes a frog; the frog becomes three stick figures scrawled across the sky. I watch our single sun drop. Beyond the water, a tree's yellow leaves are hung like butter lamps high up near the trunk. As the sun sinks, the tree appears to be lit from the inside.

Another day. Listen, it's nothing fancy. Just a man-made pond in the center of the ranch, which is at the northern, mountainous edge of a desolate state. And it's fall, not too much different from the last fourteen autumns I've lived through here, maybe warmer at times, maybe windier, maybe rainier. I've always wondered why people sit at the edge of water and throw rocks. Better to toss stones at the car that brought you, then sit quietly.

This lake is a knowing eye that keeps tabs on me. I try to behave. Last summer I swam in its stream of white blossoms, contemplating "the floating life." Now I lie on its undulant surface. For a moment the lake is a boat sliding hard to the bottom of a deep trough, then it is a lover's body reshaping me. Whenever I try to splice discipline into my heart, the lake throws diamonds at me, but I persist, staring into its dangerous light as if into the sun. On its silvered surface I finally locate desire deep in the eye, to use Wallace Stevens's words, "behind all actual seeing."

Now wind pinches water into peaked roofs as if this were a distant city at my feet. I slide my canoe onto one of the tiny, humpbacked islands. The rind of earth at water's edge shows me where deer have come to drink and ducks have found shelter. It's not shelter I seek, but a way of going to the end of thought.

I sit the way a monk taught me: legs crossed, hands cupped, thumbs touching, palms upward. The posture has a purpose, but the pose, as it must appear to the onlooker, is a ruse, because there is no such thing as stillness, since life progresses by vibration—the constant flexing and re-leasing of muscles, the liquid pulse, the chemical storms in the brain. I use this island only to make my body stop, this posture to lower the mind's high-decibel racket.

The ground is cold. All week blasts of Arctic air have braided into lingering warmth. Sometimes a lip of ice grows outward from shore, but afternoon sun burns it back. Water rubs against earth as if trying to make a spark. Nothing.

The fountain of leaves in trees has stopped. But how weightless everything appears without the burden of foliage.

At last light, my friend the bachelor duck makes a spin around the lake's perimeter. When the breeze that sweeps up from the south turns on itself, he swims against the current, dipping out of sight behind a gold-tinged swell. Fruition comes to this, then: not barrenness but lambency.

November 1. The ducks are gone. A lip of ice grew grotesquely fast during the night and now stretches across the water. I *can't* sit. Even the desire to be still, to take refuge from despair in the extremes of diversity, to bow down to light, is a mockery. Nothing moves. Looking out across the lake is like viewing a corpse: no resemblance to the living body. I go to the house despondent. When news of the California earthquake comes I think about stillness and movement, how their constant rubbing sparks life and imposes death. Now I don't know. Now the island is like a wobbly tooth, hung by a fine thread to the earth's mantle, and the lake is a solid thing, a pane of glass that falls vertically, cutting autumn off like fingers.

A week later. It has snowed, and I'm sitting on the white hump of the island. My thrift-store canoe is hopelessly locked in ice. The frozen lake is the color of my mother's eyes—slate blue—but without the sparkle. Snow under me, ice at my feet, no mesmerizing continuum of ripples forwarding memory, no moving lines in which to write music. And yet . . .

I put my nose to the white surface of the lake. It's the only way I'll know what I'm facing. At first it looks flat and featureless but closer, I see the ice is dented and pocked, and across the middle, where the water is deepest, there are white splotches radiating arms like starfish.

At midday the barometer drops and the radio carries stockmen's warnings: high winds and snow, blowing snow in the northern mountains. That's us. Sure enough the wind comes, but it's a warm chinook. Rain undulates across the face of the mountains, then turns to snow.

In the morning I go back. Drifts dapple the lake's surface like sand dunes, and between, dead leaves fly across the ones trapped under ice. But at the north end, where the warm spring feeds in, there is open water—a tiny oval cut like a gem. Something catches my eye: a duck swims out from the reeds, all alone. Is it my bachelor duck? Around and around he goes, climbing onto the lip of ice to face the warm sun.

How fragile death is, how easily it opens back into life. Inside the oval, water ripples, then lies flat. The mirror it creates is so small I can see only a strip of mountains and the duck's fat chest bulging. I want to call out to him: "Look this way, I'm here too this autumn morning," but I'm afraid I'll scare him.

He goes anyway, first sliding into the water, then swimming anxious laps. When he takes off, his head is a green flame. He circles so close I can hear the wing-creak and the rasp of feathers. Over the lake he flies, crossing the spillway and dam bank, then up through a snowy saddle, not south as I would have expected, but northwest, in the direction of oncoming storms.

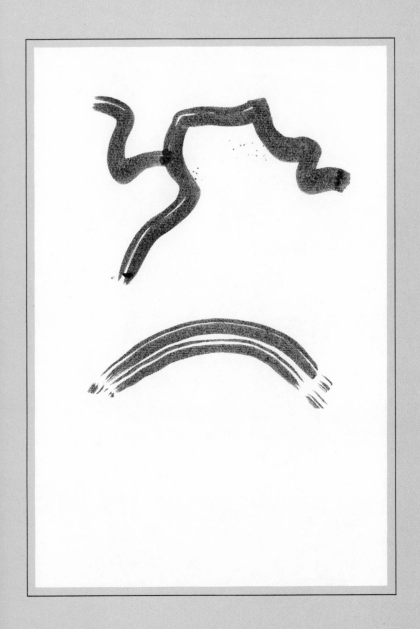

THE BRIDGE TO HEAVEN

*T*his morning I woke to the sound of crows cawing and watched light fill the room. No city noise, no sirens, no horns honking, only the distinct smell of a country not my own, the smell of straw, urine, and something sweet. From the downstairs kitchen came the sound of someone pounding *mochi*—a sticky ball made of rice, flour, and water. I am in Tokyo, and it is the day before New Year's Eve.

My friend and fellow writer Leila Philip had agreed to come along as an interpreter. All night we flew in a convex arc south of the Arctic Circle. Northern lights seemed to push out of the frozen Beaufort and Chukchi seas, whose islands of ice are crushed upward into temporary mountains, then melt down into a flat plain of ocean. Ahead was the "Country of Eight Islands," as Japan is known, whose islands were thrust up out of water in great volcanic bursts, the result of one tectonic plate sliding under the other, breaking earth's crust, allowing molten material to flow through.

Earthquakes and eruptions, seas on all sides that seem to eat the jigsaw puzzle pieces of land, islands shaped like dragons with long, twisting mountain spines, tumbling rivers, fertile plains—this is the landscape out of which the Japanese people have fashioned themselves.

I have come here to sniff out *shizen*—the Japanese word for a spontaneous, self-renewing, inherently sacred natural world of which humans are an inextricable part. I wanted to see how and where holiness revealed itself, to search for those "thin spots" on the ground where divinity rises as if religion were a function of geology itself: the molten mantle of sacredness cutting through earth like an acetylene torch, erupting as temple sites, sacred mountains, plains, and seas, places where inward power is spawned.

As we were the only guests at our Tokyo *ryokan* (inn), we breakfasted with the family. Our coffee was heated in a microwave whose trademark name was Genji—the Prince's great passion having been reduced, in this modern world, to stirring a few molecules. While we ate, the owner's father, an old farmer from Narita, with a farmer's meaty hands, fussed over the New Year's decorations, tying and retying two fern leaves around the "waist" of the *mochi* stacked one on top of the other. Looking irritated, the young owner pushed his plate away, took the dog tied to the table

leg for a walk, and came back, only to find his father had
made no progress. Impatient, he ducked into the office,
switched on the TV, and watched giant sumo wrestlers
sweat, teeter, and fall.

The old farmer smiled at me. When I asked about the
traditional hanging at the front door, he happily explained:
"The seaweed hanging down is a warrior's long hair, the
folded white paper his skirt, and the red plastic shrimp is
the samurai's armor for long life and luck." Then he added,
"But really, it is like me, only a shell, a withered old man
soon to die."

Pine for luck, straw for peace . . . the streets of Tokyo
were almost empty of cars. Little stands were going up
everywhere to sell New Year's charms: knotted ropes made
of rice straw to be hung from automobile grilles, bouquets
of white chrysanthemum mixed with fragrant pine boughs
for *tokonomas* and household shrines.

The grounds of the Asakusa Kannon Temple were
carnival-like. Throngs of people—some kimono-clad and
geta-shod—pushed down the long walkway to the entrance
of the temple, where stately pine trees, plucked whole from
the forest, were lashed to bamboo poles and tied across the
top with rice-straw ropes whose blowing tassels looked like
waves rolling in across an ocean.

Kannon is the Shinto deity of mercy and compassion.
This temple was founded when three fishermen hooked onto
a carving of the goddess in the nearby Sumida River. In the
days when Tokyo was called Edo, the temple grounds were
made popular with sake stands, restaurants, archery ranges,
and stalls where prostitutes plied their trade.

Now the side alleys offered nothing more titillating

than red-lit stands selling steamed octopus buns and a fortune-teller who prayed over New Year's charms sold by birth date. For mine, January 21, I was given a tiny plastic gourd, a red bell, and a pink plastic horse on a key ring; 1990 will be the Year of the Horse.

There are eighty thousand Shinto shrines in Japan, yet no one quite knows where Shinto comes from, since the origin of the Japanese people—thought to have migrated from two separate areas of Asia, from Malaysia and from Mongolia and China in the north—is still a matter of debate. Does Shinto derive from the Ainu of the north or from the Okinawans in the south or is it an amalgam of both?

Before the arrival of "the foreign deity," the Buddha, in 538 A.D., Shinto had no name, so integrated were the animistic beliefs within village life. And even now it is free of doctrine and dogma, since Shinto predated writing in Japan. Shinto is not a moral code or an ideology. It is, instead, a guide to natural expressions of gratitude and wonder at the substance, variety, and abundance in nature. Pines and people, thunder and monkeys, bugs and rain clouds, birds, rice, rocks, fish, foxes, and waterfalls are all *kami;* they are the gods, and the gods are manifested in them. The words *shin* and *to* mean "the way of the gods," and the dances, songs, and ritual offerings form a bridge over which the *kamisama* travel from their world to ours.

In the morning we took the Shinkansen south to Shin Kurashiki. The train's sudden speed made me feel sick. We were on our way to spend New Year's Eve watching *kagura*—sacred Shinto dances—in a small mountain shrine where a friend is the priest.

We sped through the knotty, populated heart of Honshu, past cities and factories, village houses clustered like islands within the islands of rice fields between cities, following a continuous chain of habitation. Fujiyama poked its white head up through silvery pollution, and the rivers, all diked and cement-walled, flowed, well-behaved, into the Inland Sea. Up on the banks, at golfers' driving ranges, balls slammed into huge three-sided nets under which old men fished for the New Year's special meal with ten-foot-long bamboo poles. Farmers on bicycles hooked shopping bags to handlebars and forded the shallow parts of riverbeds, then rode the grid of paths through flooded rice fields. Mountains rose to the west as hills of bamboo bowed down to the bullet train's slipstream, and small cities with their Las Vegas–style facades—bright, glittering, impermanent—were backed by villagelike residential streets, welcoming because of their human scale.

We were met at Shin Kurashiki *eki* (station) by a cabdriver who had grown up with Kanzaki-san, our host. No need to worry about finding us. We were usually the only two blondes around. Up the Takahashigawa River we went on a twisting mountain road to the village of Bisei-cho, whose name the children said meant "beautiful stars."

Bisei-cho was once a way station for samurai making their requisite journey to Edo every two years, and not much about the village had changed in six centuries. The farmhouse where we were greeted by Kanzaki-san and his family—parents, sister, brother-in-law, wife, and children—was capacious, set apart from the rest of the village on a hill next to the Shinto shrine. Only recently had the traditional open-hearth-style kitchen been given an electric stove and the thatch roof replaced with a metal one, but even so, the luxury of heat or running water was absent, in keeping with strict samurai code. The priesthood is inherited from father to eldest son, but Kanzaki-san, now a forty-four-year-old sophisticate living near Tokyo and an anthropologist by profession, commutes by bullet train to give services at this tiny shrine. By his world-weary look, I suspected he didn't always relish the duty, and when we exchanged presents, as is customary in Japan, his face lit up only when Leila gave him a bottle of Chivas Regal.

That evening all twelve of us crowded in around the low table, our crossed legs pushed under the *kotatsu*—a quilted skirt that extends out from under the table, where a heater glows. When I asked about what we were going to see that night, about the *kagura,* I was told of its legendary beginnings when a goddess, Ame no Uzume, stood in front of a rock cave holding a spear wrapped with grass and began dancing. When I asked why she danced or what the dance was about, no one knew.

The *kagura* started at midnight; we walked to the shrine at eleven. "Look at the beautiful stars," Kanzaki-san's children kept saying, but I was more impressed by the cold. Under an old tree, women from the village served a hot rice gruel, slightly sweetened. How good it tasted in the sharp air.

"*Akemashite omedetoo gozaimasu,*" we said in greeting to one another. I added my boots to the growing pile at the bottom of steep steps and walked in, flanked by Kanzaki-san's children. Earlier, Kanzaki-san had changed from turtleneck and trousers to an elegant robe of embroidered gold silk and a high-fronted priest's hat. Seated in the dark recesses of the shrine, he was banging a small drum in a slow, monotonous rhythm.

The room filled with villagers; we sat knee-to-knee on tatami. A cold wind blew in from the open, wall-less front of the shrine. No fancy-dress kimonos here—only padded jackets and trousers. Two toothless *obasan*—an affectionate term for old women—squeezed in around the one kerosene heater with a priest and warmed their hands. The village barber, the postmaster, the grocer, and the cabdriver came in as Kanzaki-san's drumbeat droned on. A prayer was chanted, offerings of food made; then we turned from the altar to the front of the room, where a young priest was positioning a huge drum. Outside, in the cold, I could see the masked *kagura* players—local farmers who had been rehearsing for months. At the last moment a girl, clutching a miniature dog with bows tied in its hair, sat down in front of me, and as she slyly took her boyfriend's hand in hers, the farmers' *kagura* began.

There were wild-eyed masks, long flowing silk robes, sword fights, and boisterous tussles with a whiskered being who looked more like a lion than a dragon; drumming and singing, sharp yells, and howls of mock misery. The play— a melodrama pantomime—went on and on. Children who had scooted to the front sat enthralled, and the *obasan* laughed heartily during every skirmish, despite the grim story line: a woman had been raped by a dragon and went insane; three old farmers took revenge, stirring up a brew of sake—à la Macbeth—to get the dragon drunk, then cut off his head.

Between each act lay priests threw food into the audience: mandarin oranges, packages of shrimp chips, candy. "Watch out," Kanzaki-san had warned us. "Last year it got wild. An *obasan* started throwing the food back at the priest." Oranges zinged by as children screamed with delight, grabbing food out of the air. A *mikan* (orange) hit me square in the forehead, juice rolling down both sides of my nose. The *obasan* hoarded their prizes in their laps.

The play continued. A wiry, shaven-headed man who wore a Parisian beret sang along during the play. He had once been one of the actors. During the third intermission the girl with the dog left, her boyfriend following obediently behind her as if he too were on a leash. By 3:00 A.M. heads bobbed with sleep—all except the children. "The beating drums bring the *kamisama* down," Kanzaki-san's son whispered. "Can you feel them yet?" I nodded, but he didn't believe me. Instead, feeling pity, he laid a small blanket across my lap.

Down the mountain, over the Inland Sea, first light shot up through clouds like pieces of steel. "*Akemashite ome-detoo gozaimasu,*" I said again as we left, pleased with myself for being able to string three Japanese words together. "It's the Year of the Horse," the children yelled, galloping down the path ahead of me toward the house. Then to bed for two hours under mounds of quilts and up again at seven for the New Year's feast.

As we squeezed in around the *kotatsu,* Kanzaki-san's eighty-year-old father began the festivities. A tiny red lacquer cup filled with sake blessed by the priests was passed around. "This is special sake. It comes from the *kami,*" Kanzaki-san explained. "You could drink this all day and never get drunk." Even so, the women only touched the liquor to their lips. When the next, slightly larger cup was passed, Kanzaki-san's son accidentally took a gulp. Everyone laughed. When the cup went around again, Leila made reference to the "strong drinkers" in Wyoming. Kanzaki-san smiled. "A strong drinker in Japan is called a cat who has become a tiger," he said, eyeing his son sternly as he took another gulp. He was the eldest son, and I wondered if he was in line to become a priest.

Later Kanzaki-san confided, "If that's going to happen, he has to start studying now . . . and that would interfere with his baseball practice."

When the sacred sake was gone, our cups were filled with the ordinary stuff. Secular sake? I asked. We picked through dish after dish of New Year's food: fermented soybeans, fish eggs, pork, wild boar, rice, and a huge, freshly caught fish.

On the train going north that afternoon, I felt myself drifting away from the beginning of 1990 like a skiff passing a lighted buoy. Out the window that sentinel was Fujiyama, most sacred of all Japanese mountains, pure *kami* from timberline to caldera, gleaming in winter sun. Mountains are central to Shinto. The sea-surrounded, alpine landscape shaped religious acts. When Buddhism, with its philosophy of transience, fused with Shinto, religious pilgrimage through mountains expanded a sense of sacredness from specific temple sites to the entire geography—wherever the pilgrim's feet happened to land. The journey was life, life was journey, and the transience of life stood for the process of spiritual transcendence as embodied, literally, by physical movement. Geography became internalized: the farther the sojourner walked from discursive mind and habitual thought, the closer she or he came back to original nature, to the "Buddha nature" within. The word "walk" in Japanese can also refer to Buddhist practice.

For most of my life I have thought of my home state of California and Japan as two jigsaw pieces once joined in the same puzzle. I know they were not, but something of the spirit of both landscapes makes me think they were. The coasts and mountains of each have become occasions for sojourns.

Leila and I travel north to the sacred, snowy mountains of Tōhoku, which is how the Japanese refer to northern Honshu. Remote, rugged, mountainous, wintry, the region is their frontier, their Siberia. It is the area where Matsuo Bashō wrote his famous *Oku No Hosomichi,* his *Narrow Road to the Deep North;* in its northeast corner is Osorezan, where the dead spirits of Japan live; it is the home of *itako,* women who communicate with the dead. Enclosed by the Sea of Japan and the Pacific Ocean, it gets snow continually for six months, and its long spines of white mountains look weightless in cloud.

At Kisagata we are on Matsuo Bashō's trail. In *Oku No Hosomichi* he wrote of this place: "I followed a narrow trail for about ten miles, climbing steep hills, descending rocky shores, or pushing through sandy beaches, but just about the time the dim sun was nearing the horizon, a strong wind rose from the sea, blowing up fine grains of sand, and rain too began to spread a gray film of cloud across the sky so that even Mount Chōkai was made invisible."

Out the window, Siberia pushed waves into the Japan Sea, and the ocean broke against bent pines; pines leaned into receding foam, foam washed over snow. "Path is goal, goal is path," that is what the Buddhists say. Bashō's *nikki no michi*—diaries of the road—were reminders of the ongoing spiritual process of the pilgrimage. Bashō had studied the Buddhist teachings with a Zen monk named Butchō, and the title of his book suggests a Buddhist influence. *Hosomichi* means "narrow path," a term that also alludes to the Hinayana path of Zen, the narrow way in which rigorous physical discipline leads to awakened mind. *Oku* has many meanings: "deep," "inner," "interior," "the heart of a mountain," "the inmost depths of the mind," as well as "a distant shrine."

Ahead were the Dewa-Sanzan, three sacred mountains of the north, where, for a thousand years, monks and wandering ascetics called *yamabushi*—mountain warriors—had engaged in severe practices on the slopes of Haguro, Gassan, and Yudono. Wobbly-legged pine trees leaned out toward rough water, and I thought of Japan's divine creation by the two gods Izanagi and Izanami, who stood on the floating bridge of heaven thrusting their penis-shaped spears into and out of the ocean until the drops that formed at the spears' tips coagulated and fell, forming the first of the eight main islands, Awaji, then the next, Kyushu and Shikoku, then Honshu—all the smaller ones rising out of the salty foam.

I looked for the nature that lay deep inside the landscape, its workings and rhythms, wishing I had walked as Bashō had, but all I could do was name things: *matsu, taiyō, awa, yuki.* No verbs propelled me forward over iron rails; path and goal backed up inside my feet like welders' sparks, blinding, burning every time I touched down.

At Tsuruoka *eki* we were met by a friend of a friend: a theatrical agent with pursed lips and dyed hair, whose entire job consisted of escorting us twenty-five feet from the station lobby to the bus stop, where we caught number 5 for the mountain village of Haguro. There we would be met by his friend's friend, who would give us a place to stay.

The entrance to the pilgrims' village of Haguro is marked by a vermilion torii, signifying sacred ground. Up from the checkerboard rice fields of the Shōnai Plain our gradual ascent began. Haguro is not an ordinary town, with shops, restaurants, and bars, but a way station for pilgrims who are climbing the Dewa Mountains.

The bus stopped in the middle of the village, where a man was waiting for us. Small, deep-voiced, he growled with disbelief at the weight of our luggage, filled with books and presents. We followed his banty-rooster stride through deep snow, with no idea where we were going, what arrangements had been made for us.

The houses looked like chalets. Shrubs and fruit trees were wrapped in woven straw to protect them from snow and cold. An old man passed us wearing an alpine hat and a fox fur around his neck. TV antennas stuck out from thatched roofs.

Down a narrow side street we were led into a pilgrims' inn, empty during the holidays, and we were, once again, the only guests. Upstairs we were given two large rooms with a view of the sacred mountains and felt giddy with our unexpected comfort. Before we could clean up, Ota-san, the diminutive owner of the inn, who had met us at the bus stop, pushed his head through the door: "Could I come in and drink sake with you? I've never talked to an American before," he said in Japanese.

Before we could speak, he plunked himself down on

the floor, and the beer, sake, tea, and food began coming. We were served a wonderful stew called *oden,* with potatoes, bits of meat, and fish. Sake flowed nonstop. After her fourth trip to our room, we begged Ota-san's wife to join us.

Big-boned, with a wide, amiable face, she told us she was a cousin from Hokkaido, that her marriage to Ota-san had been arranged. In turn, they had negotiated their son's marriage into the same family. Now their son worked at the shrine on top of Haguro Mountain, as Ota-san had, and he helped his wife at the inn. During the summer, pilgrims come by the coachload—forty at a time, three buses a week.

Being inn owners, they had never traveled outside their own prefecture, until last winter, when they went on a tour to Hawaii with eighty other villagers. "We were so scared, we brought a suitcase of our own food. The food there was too rich. Made us sick. There was nothing to do. Speaking English was like having something stuck between your teeth. At night the women went shopping, and the men stayed in their rooms and played cards."

Ota-san toasted us with more sake; we were the first Americans to sleep in his inn, and one could speak Japanese, at that! When I asked him how long his family had lived in Haguro, he thought for a moment: "Seventeen centuries. We were here when Matsuo Bashō came through."

Early in the morning Ota-san's son, Hajime, took us to the top of the village, where the forest lands protected by the shrine begin. The pilgrim's path to the top of Haguro-san consists of a thousand and some stone steps almost straight up the side of the mountain. But you have to descend before you go up: through a large torii, down snowy steps, through a virgin forest of cedars whose great trunks rose branchless for the first thirty feet, so that the shaggy, cinnamon-barked trees looked like columns or spires.

I walked toward the sound of water. At the bottom of the draw, a small waterfall tumbled over a rock wall. Birds sang—some kind of swallow, Hajime said. The stream flowed past three tiny shrines called *ohiraidojinga,* whose weather-beaten frames protected carved images of Shinto deities. The path led me over a narrow red bridge, then upward to the top of the mountain.

There are a few places in the world whose beauty is so complete that even words, a bow, clasped hands, seem presumptuous. I walked past an ancient, snow-covered pagoda, to the site where Bashō and his friend Sora had camped for the night. Looking back toward the waterfall and the red bridge, I thought the place so beautiful it was itself a prayer.

"We don't have time to climb these steps now," Hajime-san said, interrupting my reverie. He stooped down to reclose the Velcro straps of his winter tennis shoes. "Besides, there's a storm coming and you'll get lost and we'll be late for the food-blessing ceremony."

Matsuo Bashō climbed Haguro on June 3, 1689, then Mount Gas-san and Mount Yudono. Three hundred years, six months later to the day, we were driven to the top in a priest's blue Toyota. Bashō wrote: "This shrine on Haguro is counted among the three most sacred shrines of the north, together with the shrines on Gas-san and Yudono. . . . There are hundreds of places where the priests practice religious rites with absolute severity. Indeed, the whole mountain is filled with miraculous inspiration and sacred awe. Its glory will never perish as long as humans continue to love the earth."

Up the paved road we sped, skiers sliding down the slopes below, and, beyond, obscured by clouds, the peaks of Gas-san and Yudono, mountains so sacred a pilgrim is not supposed to write of what he or she experiences there.

A pilgrim knows that he must become a foreigner in his own life. Walking emulates spiritual progress; physical exertion is the literal way one can strip away personal armor, the disguises comfort and reference points provide. Of his climb, Bashō wrote: "I tied around my neck a sacred rope made of white paper and covered my head with a hood made of bleached cotton and set off with my guide on a long march of eight miles to the top of the mountains. I walked through mists and clouds, breathing the thin air of high altitudes and stepping on slippery ice and snow, till at last, through a gateway of clouds, to the very paths of sun and moon, I reached the summit."

On top, snow came down in thick, fat flakes. Five or six temples made up the complex, plus a huge parking lot lined with souvenir shops and *soba* stands where one could eat soup and noodles and drink special bitter tea. The main shrine was a vast, thatch-roofed, red-pillared structure. Inside, shoes removed, we padded around on thick red carpets and gazed out through a wall of windows that gave onto massive trees, sweeping mists, snow swirling down into the cedar cathedral.

Every shrine has its own foundation legend. "Opening" a temple site means discovering and releasing its latent power. It shows up as a "thin spot" that tickles the feet of the wandering priest. Haguro was "opened" by Shoken Dai-

bosatsu, a young prince who had taken vows and was es-
caping his father's assassins. He was led by a three-legged
bird he had dreamed about and wandered hundreds of miles
to the top of Haguro.

In almost all preindustrial cultures, mountains have
been venerated. They are thought to be the axial pillar of
the universe. With their special brews of violent weather,
they seem otherworldly. But at the same time, mountains
are providers: they catch clouds, shed water, give refuge,
cleanse the spirit. Standing up straight, they seem to represent the highest spiritual attainment of the human; they
are the natural sacred site on whose summits we express
our gratitude and awe.

Hajime-san excused himself while he changed into
priest's garb: a *hakama* and a white silk shirt. Then we
followed him down a long hall, up steep steps into the
freezing-cold shrine room. Incense wafted by. After a while,
fifteen or twenty monks and priests filed in, wearing white
tabi socks. Their diaphanous silk robes gave the effect of
men floating. After a prayer, priests carried food on black
lacquer trays: on one sake; on another three eggs, followed
by three carrots tied together, then a trout, its head and tail
positioned by bamboo sticks to make it look as though it
were jumping.

Purity, fertility, growth, abundance, cleanliness, and
renewal are at the center of Shinto rites. Each tray was
carried up steep steps to an altar, then brought down again
and handed from monk to priest to monk, and finally carried
out of the shrine room. After the ceremony we were ushered
to a large waiting room and served tea.

"A storm hugs the cedars of a thousand ages," Bashō

wrote. We watched a blizzard blast the great trees white. A *yamabushi* monk appeared at the door. Round-faced, stocky, unshaven, unwashed, he sat with us and drank tea. A *yamabushi*'s dress is distinct: a blue and white checked jacket over white pantaloons, pilgrim's sandals made of rice straw, a small black cap suspended in the middle of the forehead by a plastic string. *Yama* means "mountain," and *bushi* means "warrior." These are ascetic mountain monks associated with the Shugendo sect—a blend of Shinto and Tendai Buddhism—whose practices are particularly severe.

I asked the obvious: "Why did you become a *yamabushi*?"

He gave a jovial laugh. "I'm a construction worker from Sendai. I guess I was fooling around too much, and my mother told me I better straighten up, so I came here."

"Have you straightened up?" I asked.

He laughed. "I don't know. All I *do* know is that now I've lost my job."

"Are the *yamabushi* practices hard?"

"Yes."

"How hard?"

He shrugged his shoulders and laughed again. Laughter is what you are left with after you strip everything away. For more than a thousand years these three mountains and their valleys have been linked with extremes of religious practice. Long fasts, continuous pilgrimages, cold- and hot-water austerities, sword-climbing, fire-walking, flying, making oneself invisible, and self-mummification—this is what the *yamabushi* are known for.

"Does the divine dwell in the mountain?" I asked.

"Yes."

"Does the mountain dwell inside the human being?"

"Yes," he replied.

In Buddhist-Shinto cosmology, Haguro, or any sacred mountain, is both heaven and hell, the dwelling place of the *kamisama* and the dead. Its slopes are layered, like mushrooms on a tree, with hot hells and cold hells and various paradises with jeweled trees and waterfalls as tall as the cosmos—like the Tibetan *bardos* through which the journey of life and death is taken.

"How many straw sandals have you worn out getting here?" I asked.

"It's not the sandals I care about . . . it's my feet."

"How many feet, then?"

Intensely physical, the severe *yamabushi* practices are also mimetic: when the *yamabushi* climbed a ladder of swords, he was enacting the difficult ascent to heaven and enlightenment; when pouring hot water on himself, he was going through the *bardos* of hell; walking over fire, he was showing he had become an empty vessel to absorb human suffering. These practices are a warrior's rituals, the simplified life and sharp leaps of fearlessness jettisoning him into an awakened state.

The "tree-eating" Mount Yudono monks engaged in fasts of one thousand to four thousand days, which ended in a self-mummified death by starvation. Their restricted diet of nuts, berries, tree bark, and pine needles was gradually reduced over the days, then diminished to almost nothing—one pine needle, one berry. At this point the internal organs simply emptied out, and what was left was skin stretched over bones. Sitting in lotus position at death, they were buried for three years, then disinterred, dressed in an abbot's robes, and are now displayed in glass cases.

Outside, we listened to the *yamabushi* blow his conch shell. The snow had stopped. In the distance I could see parts of Gas-san and Yudono but could only guess at their actual shapes and the mysterious practices that went on there. The sound of the conch was wild and melancholy. Dōgen, the founder of the Sōtō Zen sect, had said that body and mind must drop away in order for one to fuse oneself with the body and mind of the universe. The Mount Yudono monks had taken the idea literally. Now some skeptics say the Haguro monks are "postcard *yamabushi,*" not serious practitioners, here only for tourists. Who is to know? Just as the deep, oceanic notes subsided, a boxcar-sized slab of snow slid from the temple roof directly behind us. The *yamabushi* did not flinch, and I saw a corner of his mouth lift in a smile.

On our last morning in Haguro we drank tea with Mr. and Mrs. Ota. Hajime and his wife had gone to visit friends, and the elder Otas were lonely. Incense drifted across the TV screen, which showed a Japanese couple visiting Paris in the spring.

When it was time to meet the bus, Ota-san hefted our luggage into a wheelbarrow, and I asked him if it had gotten any lighter. He tipped his head to one side and sucked in breath between clenched teeth. As he rolled the wheelbarrow out onto the snowy road, Mrs. Ota gave me a pair of *waraji,* pilgrim's sandals. "There are the last ones. The sandalmaker died just before Christmas, and there is no one to replace him." Leila carried the gourd-shaped bottle of *o-miki,* a rice liqueur, blessed by the priests at Haguro Shrine. As we sped down the mountain, crossing the Mogami River onto the Shōnai Plain, I thought of the river of gifts that pass through hands in this country: from prefecture to prefecture, from priest to pilgrim to priest.

We gave the *o-miki* to Yamagouchi-san, the young priest who met us at Morioka *eki,* because he had gone on a *yamabushi* retreat with Hajime Ota in Haguro. When we arrived at the temple, a service for the prosperity of a new business was just ending. Suited men and women were slipping into their city shoes, and priests were stripping off robes in the shrine room, making lecherous remarks about Leila and me, thinking we could not understand.

Out in front of the temple, white chickens picked through gravel where the New Year's food stands had been. Yamagouchi-san explained that they were kept here because a crowing rooster was the helpmate of Amaterasu, the goddess of the sun, when she brought light to the world, and the statue of a white horse wearing pilgrim's sandals belonged to the *kamisama* who rode white horses while visiting the human realm.

Tall, sweet-faced, earnest, Yamagouchi-san was eager to talk. Over dinner at his best friend's restaurant, on the temple grounds, he told us he had been born near Morioka and had always wanted to be a priest. "It is the best thing in the whole world to be," he exclaimed, his face growing crimson from sake. "Because the priest is the go-between between the people and the *kamisama.* The only way to come closer to the *kami* is to be one yourself."

This sent his friend into hysterical laughter. "I'd rather eat and drink," he said, raising his glass cheerfully.

When our food came, Yamagouchi-san grew serious. "During training on Haguro, you don't get much to eat.

My body became very light. Afterward I understood how much I owe to the *kamisama*."

"It helps to have a friend with a restaurant too," his friend quipped.

"I couldn't be happy doing anything else. When you go into a forest, your feelings change, don't they? Because that is where the *kamisama* live. In the spring, when the cherry trees blossom, we feel so grateful, so happy, and we all drink sake to celebrate."

"We're happy in the winter too," his friend said, filling our cups again. The more sake Yamagouchi-san drank, the gentler his voice became. I liked the lovely innocence of his face. Children are thought to be *kami* until the age of seven. Yamagouchi-san said it was the duty of a Shinto priest to recapture that childlike state: to be spontaneous and passionate, fresh-minded and free.

"Scientists go to the moon and say, 'This is what is real,' but we Japanese think that is a superficial view. Even if our culture is changing fast, our hearts stay the same. We want to live where we were born; we want to die on tatami. The sun shines and the rice grows, and that is the power of the *kamisama!*"

Yamagouchi-san had said that priests are the go-betweens for the people and the *kamisama; itako* go between the living and the dead. Early the next morning we were on our way to the northeast corner of Honshu to meet the *itako,* mediums who go into trance and communicate with the dead. We would also climb Osorezan, the lone mountain where all the dead spirits of Japan reside. I bought coffee from a cart going through the train, amused by the segregation of

Western-style snacks from Japanese and the fact that the honorific *o* is used only before Japanese foods.

Out the window, Iwateyama, "the Fuji of the north," rose abruptly from fields where rice straw had been tied in bundles like conical hats or smaller mountains paying homage at Iwate's feet. Everything I saw seemed imbued with the *kamisama:* the unplanted rice fields and the little gardens where winter vegetables—cabbages and scallions—had been bruised and blanched white by the cold. Even the old food vendor pushing his cart through the train chanted: ". . . *bentō-ni* . . . *o-cha* . . . *bentō-ni* . . . *o-cha* . . ." in a voice as sweet and clear as a priest's.

Passing through a knot in the Ōu Mountains, snow flew. Water ran between thick hips of snow as we crossed over a gorge on an iron bridge that shuddered with the train's weight. In this island culture, bridges occur everywhere in the literature. The frequent necessity of crossing water has come to stand for the pilgrim's journey from this world to the next, from samsara to nirvana. *"Yume no uki-hashi"* in *The Tale of Genji* alludes to the tenuous romantic ties between men and women as well as the ghostly ones between the realms of the living and of the dead. Impermanence figures so strongly in Asian religions: I wondered if it might not have evolved from a geography where islands rise precipitously out of the ocean and the earth shudders under everyone's feet.

As the train pushed down from the mountains toward the Pacific Ocean I read this poem by Fujiwara no Teika:

The bridge of dreams
floating on a spring night

soon breaks off:
parting from the mountaintop,
a bank of clouds in open sky.

An anthropologist, Toshimi Sakuraba, was to meet us
at the station, but since he didn't show up, we walked to
the sprawling, Disneyland-like spa—an *onsen*—where his
folklore museum was housed. A friend of Kanzaki, our New
Year's Eve host, he met us at the front desk, and after
arranging for rooms, we followed him on a whirlwind tour
of indoor Japanese *onsen* kitsch. Mile-long hallways con-
nected football-field-sized dining rooms; public baths gave
way to entertainment centers loud with high-decibel video
games. Couples on holiday strolled by in *yukata* and flip-
flops, with damp towels over their arms. Small and serious, our guide moved so fast we had to run to keep up
with him.

Down in the basement were the dank rooms of the
Misawa folkcraft museum. After exhibits of farming and
fishing tools, ancient weavings, and pottery, we found ourselves in front of a photographic exhibit of *itako* in trance
on top of Osorezan.

Itako are not considered true shamans, because they are
not called by a dream spirit and led to strange mountaintops,
nor are they suddenly possessed from within. A woman
becomes an *itako* because she is blind; blind men become
masseurs. Before braille, these were the only professions
deemed possible for a person without sight.

Despite the practical aspect of an *itako*'s calling, her
apprenticeship is long, beginning when she is twelve or
thirteen. Innate talents and motives vary, but it is said almost

universally that people who are blind possess a gift for inward vision.

In the afternoon, Sakuraba-san took us to a small farming village to meet an *itako* he had interviewed before. The museum sent a car and a driver with a wide, Mongolian face and an angular nose. When he was out of earshot Leila commented that he looked Ainu or Chinese, to which Sakuraba-san retorted, "No. We are all Japanese."

In the village of Itaya we pulled into the driveway of a well-cared-for suburban house. The *itako,* Mrs. Nakamura, met us at the door. Touching her hand to the wall, she went down on her knees and bowed deeply as we removed our shoes and handed over gifts. We followed her to a room, speckled and green, where she receives clients who come to make contact with the dead.

Middle-aged, she had a radiant smile and wore an angora sweater the color of a mustard field. She spoke in a sexy, breathless voice. "I've been blind since I was three years old, but I could see colors until I was twenty. My training began when I was thirteen. There was nothing else I could do, so I became an *itako.*"

Her husband, a rice farmer, brought in tea and oranges, then left the room. "The first time I heard an *itako* call up the dead I was scared and envious. I wanted to do it myself. A teacher was found for me, and I lived with her for two years."

When I asked if it was difficult, she said that because she was so young she was able to learn quite fast. She told us of nights of pouring cold water over her back, hours and hours of memorization and recitation of sutras, invocations, prayers, and a long, three-part *monogatari*—a tale about a young girl who falls in love with a horse; rather inexplicably, this goes with an *itako*'s training.

Between lessons, a young *itako* acts as a maid in her teacher's house, cleaning and preparing meals. Near the end of the apprenticeship, the austerities intensify: less food and sleep, more cold-water rituals, more recitations in order to go into trance and receive help from the *kamisama* to communicate with the dead.

When I asked her why women, not men, are *itako,* she thought for a moment, then said: "I think it is because women are more devoted. They can open themselves to the *kamisama* and let the spirits in. When I began, I did not want to be an *itako*. But what else was there for me to do? Now I am very pleased to be able to help people. They believe in me, and that is good."

It was late afternoon when her husband came in to turn on the light. She laughed because she had not realized it had gotten dark. I told her we were going to Osorezan in a day or two. "I have never seen that mountain," she said. "But I have been there." She said she went to the mountain every year in July and again in October with the other *itako*. "We walk up the mountain together. It takes a long time because we never know where we are. That's how it is when the blind lead the blind. As soon as I get to the top I can hear the young spirits crying. We line up, and people come to us. The trance lasts about ten to fifteen minutes. I can't remember what the spirits say; I let them go on as long as they want. But if it is a young one I am calling back, I feel a tingling down my spine and a heaviness."

Just before we left, she leaned close to me and whispered: "The dead spirits live in back of the mountain. Don't go there, especially at night. If you do, you won't come back."

That night Sakuraba-san took us to one of the *onsen*'s dining rooms, where the food was terrible. He didn't bother to eat. As soon as the table was cleared, we went to one of the in-house bars and ordered the whiskey. For a while he flirted with the hostess, but she had eyes for someone else. Then he wanted Leila and me to sing. It was the kind of bar that offers an open mike, with a backup tape of any popular song. The barmaid shoved a list of possibilities before us. We found a Beatles song we thought we could manage, but when she opened the case, the tape was gone. By then Sakuraba-san was tipsy, his cool anthropological demeanor gone.

A little sheepishly, he said, "The museum makes me use that driver because I get drunk every night and they're afraid I'll kill someone." He looked around for a barmaid. It was near closing time, and she already had her arms around a good-looking young man with big biceps. "My wife is away," he said. Pale and disheveled, he gave the barmaid a rueful look as we went to our separate rooms.

The next day we visited an *itako* in a village whose name I never knew. She lived in a falling-down, tin-roofed shack. A blind man answered the door and let us in. He showed us to a room with an earthen floor covered with crude straw mats. The smell of cat piss and human piss was breathtakingly strong. A door slid open on uneven rails, and a small hunchback woman with dark glasses crawled in on her knees. Her short, curly hair was held by a hair net, and she was missing a front tooth. "My house was once an old shrine. When the priest died, an *itako* came to live here. I had known her for a long time, and when she died, I took her place."

The room looked unvisited. A huge altar took up the entire back wall. Strips of silk brocade were so dirty it was hard to distinguish any color at all. A four-foot-high candleholder in the shape of a ginkgo leaf stood on the floor next to a large drum. "This is the shrine of the Agurasama," she said, putting on a white robe over a moth-eaten cardigan.

She threaded her rosary between her fingers and began rubbing them together. When she sang, her voice was beautifully clear. "At Osorezan the spirits go over the bridge and out into the lake. People say they see them . . . but I am blind. Sometimes they sing."

Then she drummed as she talked, right hand over left. "All the *itako* are dying," she said. "I don't know what will happen when we are all gone. The spirits will be in trouble. They will be lonely without us. They will have to return to the place of the dead, to hell, and no one will call them home. No young people are becoming *itako*. I've never had a student. I'm eighty years old, and no one has ever come to me and said she wants to go between the living and the dead."

In Hirosaki, Leila and I visited an *itako* who lived in a caretaker's shack behind the Shinto cemetery. Following a snowy footpath up a hill, we walked through half an acre of mortuary stones to get to her house. We knocked, and a tiny woman in her seventies, bent almost double by osteoporosis, greeted us. Though she was blind, she wore clear glasses. There was a bruise under one eye. "*Konnichi-wa,*" she said cheerfully. Sun poured into the little room, and newspaper insulated the walls against the cold. When temple bells began to ring, she cocked her head like a bird and smiled. She had been an orphan, raised by an older brother, who wasn't kind to her. Then she married and had four children before starting her training. "It took me seven years to learn how to bring the *kamisama* down," she said, "because I was already thirty-three when I began. My teacher got very mad at me and kept telling me to quit, but I kept on. Now it has been forty-five years since I first went to Osorezan."

From her small household shrine she pulled down a square straw box and drew out her rosary, called an *irataka-juzu*. Strung between three hundred red soapberry beads were animal claws and teeth and ancient coins with square holes in the middle. She threaded them between her fingers, then stopped and turned to me. "You want me to call someone down for you, don't you," she said. I wasn't prepared for this, but I gave her the name of a loved one who had died fourteen years before. She asked me where he lived, what day and hour he had died, the cause, and what relationship he was to me. Leila translated. Holding the beads threaded between her fingers, she began rubbing them in long, swift strokes, singing, asking for the *kamisama*'s help.

She stopped suddenly. "He wasn't your husband . . . he was an 'outside' person, wasn't he?" Yes, I told her. Mistakenly, Leila had used the word "husband" instead of "husband-to-be." The *itako* nodded, then began again. Above a butane-fueled hot plate and a bucket of water with a bamboo dipper, a clock chimed eleven. A dog tied up in back growled, and snow on the tin roof began to drip, melted by sun.

Her chanting intensified, then stopped. "I can't understand him. He doesn't speak Japanese."

"He was Welsh."

"I'll try again."

The rubbing of the beads made a harsher sound. During the months just before and after David's death, I had felt something cold behind my left shoulder. Now bright sun warmed my back. She began mumbling. I looked at Leila.

"It's in some weird dialect," she whispered.

The *itako* clapped her hands, then stopped. "I can barely make him out," she said. "But he says he hasn't forgotten you. I prayed for his well-being. I'm sorry. But he's so far away. It would be easier if we were on Osorezan."

Sakuraba-san and his driver picked us up early the next morning, and we drove north five hours in bad weather up the narrow arm of the Shimokita peninsula, shaped like an ax; its blade, if lowered, would strike down through the middle of Honshu. I was filled with melancholy. The night before, I'd dreamed about my dead friend. Unlike any other dream I'd had of him, he wasn't about to die, nor was he already dead: we had infinity before us.

Rain swept across the road in gray sheets, lifting off and blowing back into seawater. In the town of Noheji we passed a hearse. Its ornate, gilded frame curved out over the body of the truck on which it had been built. From there to Mutsu there were no towns, only fishing camps where boats were pulled up on beaches and turned over on snow. Small torii faced weather-beaten shrines where offerings were still made "for luck in fishing." Rain turned to sleet. The driver put on a tape of an *itako* chanting. The sky, sea, and the snow-covered shore were all the same gray color.

An old woman with a curved spine slogged through a dairy farm in gum shoes, dragging the pointed end of an umbrella across the ground.

A waitress in Aomori had warned us: "If you go to Osorezan, the spirits will attach themselves to you and go down the mountain on your back. Be careful. If you let them do this, you'll suffer sickness. When you go there you have to be strong and not let them in." Aomori is the place where the word for dying also means "going to the mountain." I looked ahead to where the mountain, Osorezan, should have been, but all I saw were particles of snow bombarding us as if the mountain had blown apart.

At Mutsu we stopped for lunch. Our driver didn't want to have anything to do with Osorezan; he only wanted to eat and read the comic books the restaurant provided. Our young waiter's sweatshirt had these words, in English, printed on the back: "O. Henry. His stories are famous for their urbane ironies and unexpected twist at the end."

By the time we had finished eating, it was snowing hard. At the north end of town, where the road to Osorezan began, an iron gate swung across our path. The snow was too deep. Sakuraba-san looked crestfallen. All this way for nothing. But I had not come partway around the world just to be turned back by a gate. "We'll walk," I said. It would be a twenty-six-mile round trip. Sakuraba-san gave me an incredulous look, but when he saw there was no choice, he borrowed the driver's galoshes and set off up the mountain ahead of us.

The road to Osorezan is not narrow but deep. Deep with snow, thick with forebodings, silent, inward, trackless. We

started up through a dense forest, an island of wild vegetation in a country where rice fields dominate the ground.
On either side of the road thick stands of cedar, pine, and
cherry were twined with the vines of wild grape like "red
threads," a Japanese term that alludes to passion. I remembered a poem from Genji:

> Longing for the one
> Who crossed over
> The mountain of Death,
> I gaze at tracks
> And wander lost.

Ankle-deep at first, the snow was heavy as cement.
Behind us, our tracks filled in quickly, so that our ascent
left no trace, and I wondered if that was how it was when
you died. I'd worn too many clothes and began sweating.
"People walk to heaven," Sakuraba-san said, pausing to look
at the sky, then passing me again. I wondered what Shinto
heaven looked like, if it differed from Buddhist heaven. I
wondered if the dead do walk, what they walk on, and if,
like Dante, they have a guide.

Osorezan's Ainu name means "Dreadful Mountain."
It is an eye in the head of the ax, staring into the closed
eyes of humans cut down by death; once a fiery volcano, it
too is dead. I slogged up its slopes, its rivers falling away
from my feet. Every two hundred yards or so, we passed a
statue of Kannon, the deity of mercy and compassion. "I
pray to Kannon every morning," the *itako* Mrs. Nakamura
had said, and I wondered how many prayers it took to get
up this mountain blind.

As the road steepened, Sakuraba-san upped the pace. Finally, we stopped at a spring and drank thirstily from a bamboo dipper left on a rock for pilgrims. The snow was now up to my shins. We crossed one animal track all day— that of a serow, a wild sheep protected in Japan. That was all. The sky, like an iron plate, lowered on my head.

Near the top the road wound down to the caldera before flattening out into a wide plain. Wind gusted, carrying the smell of sulfur. Pools of hot water, orange and green, bubbled out of the ground. We passed a ramshackle, seedy *onsen,* boarded up for the winter. A child's pink bike lay on its side in the ooze. I walked on. When the steam and the cold mist lifted, I could see across a broad lake, whose ice-dappled emerald waters filled the volcano's crater.

Osorezan has its own cosmology. The beaches are called *gokuraku-gahama,* which means "Beach of Paradise." The tumbled, sulfur-stained rocks are the site of one of Osorezan's hells. Beyond is the "Pond of Blood"—now white with snow—where the journeyers must drink, another one of the hundred and thirty-six hells where relatives of the dead pray.

Ahead was a narrow red bridge, the one the *itako* had told me about. It connects *higan* and *shigan*—this shore and the other shore—and the dead spirits must cross it before taking up residence on the water.

I walked over the Taiko Bridge and continued on. Ahead, in the mist, I could make out the temple, Bodai-ji. As we approached its high gates, four ravens appeared out of the forest, cawing. Greetings! I cawed back. Leila and I rested on the steps, because the gates to the temple were locked. Twelve hundred years ago a priest, Jokaku Daishi, studying Buddhism in China, had a dream that he must return home. From Mount Hiei near Kyoto, he began to walk. He had been directed to a mountain in the northeast corner of Honshu. Thirty days later he reached Osorezan and fasted. Finally, the "thin spot" revealed itself, "opening" so the holiness could come through; on that spot he built this temple.

Inside there is a carving, left by the priest, of Jizo, the savior of those lost in the *bardos*. Every night Jizo walks these grounds, gathering up the ghosts of dead children. Believers say the edge of his robe is wet from the children's tears and that the walking stick carried in his right hand is hot to the touch. Sai no Kawara is the beach in front of the temple, where children, chased by demons, are saved by him.

After eating an orange, we walked to a building where smoke was coming from a chimney. Two leathery-faced old caretakers came out, shocked to see they had visitors, and Americans at that. Timidly, they invited us in. Two caged doves cooed as I unlaced my boots. Inside, a television was showing a Mickey Mouse cartoon dubbed in Japanese. We sat on red cushions around a wood stove and drank tea from big, handleless mugs.

The caretakers, both in their late seventies, looked more Chinese than Japanese, with their dark skin, high cheekbones, and easy smiles. They had been on the mountain since September. It was now January, and we were their first visitors. Both had been born in Mutsu, the town where we'd had lunch, and, as bachelors, had traveled in labor camps to Tokyo and Yokohama as construction workers. Now they were too old to work and had taken this job. "We come up when the people are leaving and go down when they come up," the older of the two said.

Through a doorway I could see a large table heaped

with cabbages, onions, and carrots, fifty-pound sacks of rice, and stacks of eggs. "We don't like each other's cooking, so we cook for ourselves," one of them said, as if the results could be that different, given the ingredients.

After tea, they refilled our cups with instant coffee. We offered them a crumpled American candy bar, which they refused. I asked them if they were afraid to live here. The older one shrugged, no. But the younger of the two said he heard dead people crying at night and saw them moving around, legless, on the shore of the lake. "They glide on air like birds. I don't know why they don't have legs," he said.

I noticed Sakuraba-san checking his watch. It was after four when we rose to leave. "You better stay the night; it will be dark in half an hour," the younger one said. "No, no, we must go," Sakuraba-san protested, stepping into his galoshes. The caretakers followed, showing us where on the temple grounds the *itako* do their work. "Sometimes we come back up in July, just to see the *itako*," they said. "The caretaker who was here before us died here. His spirit didn't have to go anywhere. It was already home."

More than a foot of snow had fallen since we had started up, and the walk back, which I had expected to be easy, was just as laborious. A little way from the temple, I stopped and turned. The two old men, who looked as if they belonged in the Tang dynasty, smiled sweetly and waved goodbye. Around the lake, over the Taiko Bridge, up the lip of the crater, then down in steep snow and dark. *"Oku . . . oku . . . oku . . ."* The word came with the rhythm of each step. This was my narrow road to the deep north, my walk to a distant shrine, my inward journey, my penetration of darkness.

The day before, I had asked Sakuraba-san if he believed in *itako,* if he believed Osorezan was a place of spirits, and he had said, "No, not really." But now because it was dark, he passed me with a frightened look and began running down the mountain. I did not try to keep up.

Singing to myself, I shook my shoulders every now and then to see if there were any spirits clinging to my back. Nothing. I felt light and heavy at the same time. I wondered if the *itako* we visited had really talked to my dead friend, if they actually talk to anyone, or were they simply meting out consolation at two thousand yen a shot? I didn't care. We are always looking for difficult truths in easy contexts and demanding simple answers within complicated wholes. Perhaps the gesture is enough. Like an ax coming down into a log, a gesture dents consciousness, wedging it wider. It pleased me to have found a place where disbelief could be suspended, where the mind was open, permissive, accepting, and could see worlds behind masks and sacred dances, hear voices inside the wild conch shell and the rasping rosary.

At the spring I drank deeply and bowed to the goddess Kannon, who inspires compassion. To go with suffering, to go with passion . . . that is what the word "compassion" really means. Trudging, glissading, my heels sinking deep in fresh snow, I saw that the New Year's new moon had come almost full and the road to and from Osorezan glistened white.

HOME IS HOW MANY PLACES

*W*enè *mu.* That's what the Chumash Indians called this southern California harbor: "resting place," because it was here that they waited in their high-bowed, ocean-going canoes for rough seas to subside before they paddled to their island homes. My destination is Tuqan, the Chumash name for San Miguel, the northernmost of the Santa Barbara Channel Islands, about sixty miles from here.

In the dark, I step onto the *Peace* and stow my gear. She is a sixty-five-foot diesel-powered boat fitted out for diving expeditions, though tonight she is taking twenty of us on a museum-sponsored tour. Eleven P.M. rolls around. It is usual for the Chumash to wait until at least midnight before heading out, when the seas are calmer. James, the young, dark-haired captain, stumbles into the galley, rubbing sleep from his eyes. He asks for water and glances at the clock. "Not yet," he says to no one in particular, then disappears up a ladder to his bunk because he'll be on watch all night.

The harbor is quiet, only a gentle breeze. The decks have been scrubbed down, but the bolts that hold this iron workhorse together are rusted. By comparison, the Chumash *tomol* (canoe)—used as transportation between the mainland and the islands—was constructed from driftwood shaped into planks with rock tools and sanded smooth with cloths made from sharkskin. Lashed together with milkweed fiber and sealed with black asphaltum—the tar that seeped up on Santa Barbara beaches—the *tomol* was painted ocher, its bow inlaid with abalone shells that flashed in moonlight like two eyes.

For eight thousand years or more the Chumash lived in isolation and peace. One of at least sixty tribal groups in California, they once numbered fifteen thousand. They had no neighboring enemies and no warrior cult. Personal vengeance, carried out with poisonings, was the only violence they knew. Climate, the unjust taskmaster of the Plains nations, blessed the Chumash with year-round sun and abundant food from land and sea. Tule elk, deer, and bear were hunted; mussels and abalone were plucked from rocks; acorns, seeds, and berries were gathered. They lived in a five-thousand-square-mile paradise. From San Luis Obispo south to Malibu, the Chumash nation included a chain of pristine habitable islands, a unique south-facing coastal range, inland valleys, and three hundred miles of beach.

Hardly anything would be known about these people if it had not been for John Peabody Harrington, a Smithsonian anthropologist and onetime resident of Santa Barbara. In 1912 he returned to his hometown and rented a Spartan room in the ivy-covered Riviera Hotel. He was not a young man, having already amassed 800,000 pages of notes on Native American cultures elsewhere, but the Chumash were dear to his heart.

When he sat down with Fernando Librado, Maria Ignacio, and Mary Yee—Chumash descendants—to record every remembered detail of traditional and contemporary Chumash life, Fernando was already 108 years old.

"I remember Mr. Harrington," Paulina, my friend, told me. She had grown up with Mary Yee's daughter. "He wore an old suit, always the same one. He didn't eat, he didn't sleep. He was sick, but he always worked. Every day he came to Mary Yee's house. She had married a Chinese man, but she was Chumash, and she was teaching the language to Harrington. We girls were sent out because she didn't want us to hear. She was ashamed to speak that way in front of us. But she told Mr. Harrington everything she knew."

Those notes were kept uncatalogued in eight hundred cardboard cartons in the basement of the Smithsonian until recently when the Museum of Natural History in Santa Barbara brought them home piecemeal. The resident anthropologist had to order the notes by the inch. "We didn't have much money. That's all we could afford." Now the

museum is a workshop of Chumash culture: recordings of
Mary Yee are being transcribed by her daughter, notes written in longhand are being typed and archivally stored, and
Harrington's one-of-a-kind typewriter fitted with Chumash-
language keys is on display.

Sometime after midnight, James, the young captain, reap-
peared, hair slicked back De Niro style: "Get ready to go
under way," he yelled down to the two galley cooks, Ventura
women along for the ride. "This isn't going to be an easy
night," he whispered, passing me. Then the diesel engines
revved, and we moved slowly to sea.

The moment we passed beyond the harbor's protective
breakwater, heavy winds hit. Nothing had prepared me for
the size of the swell on the outside: ten-foot waves slammed
against us as James headed the *Peace* up into the wind, her
heavy bow dropping down into troughs as new swells rose,
big as buildings.

Long after the museum people had gone below to sleep,
I sat alone on deck, holding the rail. There's no place else
I'd rather be than under way at night in a small boat. Once,
on a sailboat, I was lashed to the tiller in a sea this rough
and felt wind send shocks up through the keel and down
the mast into my hands. Now the coastline lights of Oxnard,
Ventura, and Santa Barbara receded and those of a drilling
platform loomed ahead. We seemed to move forward only
by going up and down—as if a giant were playing ball with
an elevator.

I was raised in a house in Montecito with a view of
the sea and never understood how the steel legs of an offshore
drilling platform could stand so straight in water and why,

at Christmas, the rig was made to look like a Christmas tree. Now the *Peace* chugged under the platform's city-sized deck, stacked with metal containers for living and sleeping, its cold immensity mocking us as we lunged away into the dark curvaceous violence of the sea.

The wind strengthened. I thought of Saint John of the Cross's "dark night of the soul." At least he had decent footing. I felt sudden happiness. Who cares where water stops and wind begins, or if night ever ends, or what the difference is between dream and hope and doubt and reality? There's a sameness to it all, which I relish, even as the boat stands upright on swells, walking the ladder of night, then— kabam—belly flops again. Matsuo Bashō's friend Saigyo wrote:

Since I no longer think
of reality
as reality,
what reason would I have
to think of dreams as dreams?

I lick salt water from my face. Spray blots out stars. Above, the boat's running lights are the only constellation. No celestial navigation tonight, unless it is possible to take a fix on oneself, which would mean I'd have to know where I was while still lost.

Now, instead of salt, I lick darkness from my mouth. It's said that at the bottom of the gravest doubt there is satori, and mention is made of fireflies lit up inside a grave.

Light can come into being anywhere. The boat shudders, and the captain's face, illuminated by chart lights, is a torch.

The Chumash thought the cosmos was made of three flattened disks floating in the ocean and the middle one, where they lived, was the biggest island of them all. Two giant serpents held it up. When they grew tired, their tails moved, and that is what caused earthquakes. The lower world was inhabited by *nunasis*—creatures who came out after dark. Some could swallow whole trees, while others had faces with loose, putrefying skin. The upper world was presided over by Slo'w, an eagle whose flapping wings—like bellows—caused the moon to grow full, and after, the wings were knives, cutting the moon to a sliver. The water in the streams and rivers was the urine of frogs.

I laid my bedroll between the hatch and rail on the deck behind the wheelhouse. Neither the wind nor the storm swells had diminished, but I could see stars. The Chumash called the Milky Way *suyapo'osh,* after the white insides of piñon nuts and the long trail they walked to gather them. Lying on my back, I saw the Milky Way as a rope, one I tried to grab in order to steady myself but, at the boat's highest pitch, kept missing. How was it possible to survive these seas in a *tomol?*

Every once in a while James stuck his head out the wheelhouse door to check on me. I'd climbed into my bag with shoes, clothes, and glasses on, because anything loose would have been tossed overboard. The entire boat was wet. With both hands I held on to scuppers and hatch covers. The bow of the boat was like a hand feeling the weight and shape of each swell, how and when wind shifted, from which side we were being ambushed by water. Every now and then I caught glimpses of what looked like a cozy bachelor pad behind the wheelhouse's red curtains: James enthroned in a pilot's seat covered with sheepskin; his three helpers playing cards at a table bolted to the floor; sexy music playing on a tape deck . . . then the curtains would swing closed again.

The boat tipped up and down, and fins of salt water sprayed my face. Old Fernando Librado said that at night the sun goes to rest in the hole of a sand dollar, leaving its rays outside while the sun rests within. I stuck my head under my canvas bedroll cover and smiled in delight.

Toward dawn I must have dozed off. I woke with a start because the boat had stopped shaking. The water was smooth and gray; the sky was gray. Beads of moisture dripped from my hair. Then I saw blue cliffs: Santa Cruz Island. As the sun rose from its hiding place, fog melted away.

There are four northern Channel Islands: Anacapa, Santa Cruz, Santa Rosa, and, most remote, San Miguel. Geologically, they are part of the continental borderland—what geologists call "fringing islands" as opposed to archipelagos made and cut away by rising and dropping seas, the lateral shear of tectonic plates and volcanism. Controversy still rages over whether there was a land bridge to the mainland. Regardless, early-man sites have been found on Santa Rosa dating forty thousand years ago, linking these early islanders with dwarf elephants that, land bridge or not, swam from the mainland and flourished in isolation.

The word *chumash* means "islander." The First People
were thought to have been born on Santa Cruz and radiated
out from there. Islanders spoke a different dialect from
mainlanders and danced different dances. They paddled
their *tomols* to the mainland to buy and sell goods, using
tiny shells as currency for exchange. On both island and
mainland they lived in villages, whose headman or woman
was called a *wot*. A council of officials called a *siliyik* took
care of village ceremonies and problems. The word *siliyik*
also means "whole world."

An old man called an *alchuklash* named children and
took care of the sick. They were also astronomers and as-
trologers. As soon as a newborn child moved, these *alchuklash* gave it a name. For example, those born in January
were self-willed and virtuous; the ones born in April, "when
the flowers are already in bloom," were cheerful and worked
for the community; and December's children were ecstatic,
then lethargic, then like gods in the world.

Fernando knew an old man whose star maps were
embedded with shells—one for the fall sky, one for the
winter, and so on, and their twelve-month lunar calendar
was adjusted to the solstices, when feather poles were stuck
into the earth—an umbilical connecting the human to the
natural world.

In 1542 João Cabrilho, whose Portuguese name was changed
to the Spanish, Cabrillo, took command of the exploratory
voyage along the California coast after his captain died.
When Cabrillo's two ships, *La Victoria* and *San Salvador,*
paused in the channel, the Chumash paddled out to the
strangers. They had never seen a European. Bartholeme

Ferrel, Cabrillo's diarist, wrote: "All the way there were many canoes, for the whole coast was very densely populated and many Indians kept boarding the ships. They pointed out their pueblos and told us their names."

Unknown to the Chumash, their "biggest island in the universe" was being reduced to a mere point on a much larger, imponderable map.

In 1769 more Europeans came to stay. Dispatched by King Carlos III to protect the area from Russian seal hunters, a priest and some Mexican soldiers arrived on a hot August afternoon. They had been told to build four military forts—*presidios*—as well as a chain of missions along the California coast like "beads on a rosary." Again the Chumash displayed extravagant hospitality. They entertained the men with singing and dancing so continuous the travel-weary conquerors moved to another camp in order to sleep. The Chumash didn't understand that their conviviality had been interpreted as acquiescence. Already they had been betrayed.

Fernando Librado said: "Civilization conquered the world at the point of a bayonet. There was also much money at the point of that bayonet." Chumash were lured to mission settlements out of curiosity. Horses, livestock, blacksmithing, gardening, tools—so much they hadn't seen. Some resisted contact with the whites, others let themselves be baptized and dexterously juggled two sets of beliefs for the rest of their lives.

The Chumash were taught to be masons, painters, carpenters, cooks, gardeners, vaqueros. Intermarriage was encouraged. Those who resisted "missionization" were often punished. Librado describes how: "There were two kinds of stocks in that room. One was shaped of wood to cover the foot like a shoe. . . . These pieces of wood were joined to a ring which went about the knee, and from this ring straps were attached to a belt that went around the waist of the person. Weights were fastened to the straps. As punishment, the priests would work men and women in the fields with those weighted shoes. The priests also sometimes shackled the feet of the Indians or shackled two together at the same time."

The "civilizing" presence of the Spaniards included many violations, among them the use of Indian women for sex by "celibate" priests. "They took all the best-looking Indian girls," Librado said, "and put them in a nunnery. The priest had an appointed hour to go there. When he got to the nunnery, all were in a big dormitory. The priest would pass by the bed of the superior and tap her on the shoulder, and she would commence singing. All the girls would join in, which, in the dormitory, had the effect of drowning out other sounds. While the singing was going on, the priest would have time to select the girl he wanted, carry out his desires, and come back to where the superior was. In this way the priest had sex with all of them, from the superior on down."

Though a good deal of Chumash culture was tolerated—Bear and Blackbird dances were performed on the completion of each mission building, for which the men had carried pine timbers on their backs all the way from the mountains—the elastic present of their tribal society had been transfixed. What had formerly been marked by tides, seasons, solstices, and eclipses was now splintered into hourly work schedules, ringing bells, whippings, and rapes. Food gathering, feasting, canoe building, and ceremony—the sta-

ples of Chumash life—were crimped into the leanest kind
of existence.

When Mexico declared independence from Spain in
1835 and the missions were secularized, the Chumash were
to inherit half the land and livestock. They didn't. The newly
appointed Mexican governor meted out large *ranchos* to
friends. The Indians worked on as cooks, sheepherders, ser-
vants, and vaqueros. They lived a double life: *alchuklash* by
night, Catholic ranch hand by day. One of them said: "Yes,
much from the outside has been forced on us. But inside
we change more slowly. We may wear the European's
clothes, but we do not wear all his thinking."

Midmorning on the *Peace,* and it has taken ten hours to go
sixty miles. "Kind of a long night," James said, handing me
a cup of coffee. "I cheated and took Dramamine," I told
him. "So did I," he said. The boat glided on calm waters,
with the copilot at the helm. The islands' sandstone cliffs
moved past, each island generating its own private weather
of marine mist and inland valley fog, and producing unique,
endemic species of animals and plants, and eccentric human
islanders.

When I was a child I lay in bed at night and looked
out at these islands. "There's no sense sailing to San Miguel,"
my father always said. "There's nothing out there." Sometimes when the wind shifted and blew in from the southwest
I could hear seals barking and a sound like women singing,
and I wanted to swim to San Miguel. It stood for the separateness I felt from my family, for the mystery of how
identity is formed. Now I find I can't say I am one thing
without saying I am another: as these islands are defined by

their relationship to the coast, so is my sense of aloneness rooted in the context of family and because of it. I knew the ways in which I was different, and how "the water between us" could be bridged by what we shared.

Islands are places where exchanges occur. Because the boundaries are so sharp, islands remind us of beginnings and endings, of birth and the arousal of consciousness of the evolutionary movement from water to land and air. At places of exile and island prisons like Sado or Alcatraz, waterline is a hard edge, forbidding as broken glass and high fences. We crave island holidays, hoping that within the geographical confines of an island we can, paradoxically, expand, shed old skin, reimagine ourselves.

Islands are reminders of arrivals and departures. In 1835 the last Native Americans were removed from the Channel Islands by Franciscan mission fathers on a chartered schooner inauspiciously named *Peor es Nada,* which translates "worse is nothing." By the time they reached San Nicolas Island, about thirty miles south of San Miguel, winter was coming on. The islanders were hastily gathered. When one woman discovered her child had been left behind, she jumped overboard and swam to shore. Because the storm was closing in, the captain sailed without her, intending to return in a few weeks, but the schooner, living up to its name, sank, and no one returned for her.

Eighteen years later, George Nidever, a fur trapper who had explored California with the Walker expedition and later became an early owner of San Miguel Island, set out to find "the lost woman of San Nicolas." He found fresh footprints, which led him to her shelter, made of whale ribs covered with sea grass and brush. The woman was roasting wild onion over a fire. No child was present, but she had dogs and two pet ravens. She wore a dress made from the skins of pelagic cormorants with the feathers still attached, sewn together with bone needles.

It is said she went willingly with Nidever. It was an easy passage that day, and she was welcomed at the Santa Barbara mission, baptized, and given a Spanish name, Juana Maria. But like other "wild people" who have been brought into the so-called civilized world, she did not thrive in captivity, and six weeks after her arrival, she died.

The three-mile passage between Santa Rosa and San Miguel is rough. During the night, the swells are obsidian boulders, not cut by the keel's knife from the sea but carved from the blackness above our heads. Now, in early light, San Miguel is cut from day, a blue muscle dropped and floating on water.

We pass Caldwell's Point, Nichols Point, Challenge Point, Bay Point, Hoffman Point, then cruise past Prince Island, blackened by pelagic cormorants and dotted with western gulls, and finally turn into the turquoise calm of Cuyler's Harbor. Small, most remote, most inaccessible of the Channel Islands, San Miguel is only fourteen square miles, roughly ten thousand acres and hit hard by prevailing northwesterly winds, which have made the western end the site of many shipwrecks. Its fractured shores—part volcanic, part sedimentary—split the California current, some of the water curling counterclockwise toward the mainland in cyclonic eddies, the other part breaking out into open seas.

A piece of dead whale floats by, perched on by two gulls, and sea lions bask on an island of undulating kelp, acknowledging our arrival with a blink of the eye. James drops anchor, and groups of us are rowed to shore. Who planted the three palm trees that greet us? They are not native to the island. A swallow nest hangs from a hunk of conglomerate rock: best view in the world of this white sandy beach and natural harbor.

As I walk, the palm fronds behind me come alive with finches. I kick blue mussel shells, red abalone, purple-hinged scallops, and thick slabs of jingle shells. There are spiny sand crabs, cancer crabs, and sand dollars. In which one does the sun find its resting place? Above a sandy shelf of plovers' nests is an ancient Chumash house site, much like the lone woman's—a curved depression where the whale rib house once stood.

Was this shelter occupied when Cabrillo was here in 1542? That was the year he wintered on San Miguel. Where did he live? Did he befriend the Chumash islanders, eat with them, sleep with them, fall in love? Sometime near Christmas he broke an arm or a leg and suffered gangrene; he died in January of the new year. A monument to him stands above Cuyler's Harbor.

This is the island my family wouldn't sail to because it was barren, they said, but walking up a steep trail from the beach, the one used by sheepmen who lived here long after Cabrillo's demise, I find that flowers and grasses abound. Ice plant frosts the cliffs, and there is saltbrush, native buckwheat, brome, lupine, morning glory, and coreopsis. Halfway up, I come on sea rocket, a strange flowering plant ingeniously adapted to island life because its seed pods break into two parts: one has a corky outer coating and drifts on water, enabling it to migrate to other islands, while the second pod drops close to the mother plant in order to colonize the ground nearby.

Islands are evolutionary laboratories. How did plants and animals get here? How did they fare in isolation? Did they mutate or stay the same? Get smaller or bigger? Flourish or go extinct? Now conservationists are looking at all kinds of islands, not just the ones surrounded by water but islands of vegetation in desert seas, and deserts surrounded by tundra. The biologist Paul Ehrlich warns us that "the earth is rapidly becoming a system of habitat islands surrounded by a sea of human disturbance," and as fragmentation increases, so will extinction rates. The same could be said for the islands of the psyche and the soul.

Up top, blow-out channels cut in sand by wind rib the northern end of the island, and to the south, gentle, treeless grasslands slope down to the sea. There is an eerie forest of caliche, calcium carbonate casing tree trunks, the broken remnants of two hundred years of continuous unmanaged grazing, which stripped the island of vegetation—vegetation that is now returning. Out across a grassy plain, island foxes bound, then leap in place, pouncing down on prey; in the Chumash islanders' Fox Dance, performers painted their faces and bodies with white bands, their necks vermilion, and wore headdresses made of junco feathers twined with flowers and a long braided tail weighted by a rock tied into the end. Dancers shook rattles made of mussel shells and sang about their crossings to the mainland: "I make a big step. I am always going over to the other side. I always jump to the other side as if jumping over a stream of water. . . . I make a big step."

There were Swordfish, Barracuda, Arrow, and Skunk

dances and the Seaweed Dance, performed by men and women dressed in feather skirts, their faces painted red with white dots. Mimicking the movement of kelp, they slithered and undulated and sang: "Behold me! I walk moving my brilliance and feathers. I will always endure in the future. Ailwawila hilele."

Near the Lesters' house site we stopped to eat lunch. Herbert Lester was hired by the island's owner in 1930 to live there and run sheep. He had suffered shell shock in World War I, and the owner thought island life would be soothing for his friend and his Yankee bride, Elizabeth. For twelve years they reigned as "the King and Queen of San Miguel," lived in a rambling house, "Rancho Ramboullet," made of planks salvaged from wrecked ships, had two daughters, and produced a decent sheep crop despite dry years and a deteriorating soil surface. But in June of 1942, Lester, in ill health, killed himself, and the happy island days ended.

Was it really ill health that prompted Lester to take his own life, or geographical and emotional isolation? And why did the lost woman of San Nicolas die after being brought to the mainland, or did "civilization" represent another kind of prison, which she had never encountered before?

As we rowed back to the *Peace,* I saw James leaning against the wheelhouse, mirrored sunglasses reflecting our slow progress, and thought: Islands are emblematic not only of solitude but of refuge and sanctuary, the way a small boat is an island in rough seas.

On deck, a stocky young surgeon hands me a glass of wine. "I love these islands, but I could spend days just on the color of the sea. It's so hard to hold in my mind: sometimes it's jade that's been cut, sometimes turquoise," he said.

Dinnertime. Twenty of us crowd into the galley and eat greasy chicken and limp coleslaw. A boat pulls up alongside and I hear yelling, then James falls past the porthole window. He has jumped from the wheelhouse to the deck. "You do not have permission to board," he yells. Too late. The men with badges are already roaming around. Hatches and lockers are searched, then the dining room. "It's the Game and Fish guys," someone whispers. "They're looking for illegal lobster." Relieved, I hold up a drumstick. "Would we be eating this if we had lobster?" I ask. Finally, the men depart. When their boat is gone, James appears, with a devilish grin on his face. "Okay, bring out the lobster!" Then he disappears.

Dark. The sea air is velvet against my face, a perfect temperature of seventy-two degrees. I sit on the hatch behind the wheelhouse and look across the water toward the California mainland, toward the house where I grew up, but can see nothing. No land, no lights, no eucalyptus or lemon trees. *Home is how many places?* Chumash history was not taught in California schools when I was growing up, but recently a friend with Chumash ancestry said, "If you want to know who you are and where you are, you have to know who lived here first."

Up on a rock outcrop above my parents' house, he gave me a geography lesson, naming names up and down the coast: Humaliwo, Muwu, Mitsqanaqa'n, Shisholop, Kosho, Shuku, Q'oloq, Lephew, Lisil, Mikiw—names of Chumash villages. Humaliwo—meaning "the surf sounds loudly"— is now Malibu. Tinik was near the Reagan ranch. At Montecito's Hammond estate, on whose rolling lawns I once attended all-night formal dances, condos have been built on top of a Chumash burial ground. To the north, Point Conception—where oil companies have tried to lay pipeline—is the Chumash gateway to the Land of the Dead. Nearby, Upop, a village whose name means "shelter," is now Vandenberg Air Force Base, with its new launching pad for missiles. And Shalawa—Montecito, where I was born—is haven to Hollywood's new rich. Just above the fancy houses, a hot spring was once a village called Alish'i'l. Its warm waters are now piped through my parents' house.

From the decks of the *Peace* I look down on kelp beds but see only the top of a great watery forest home. Under the golden canopy, opal-eyes, Norris's top snails, and red abalone dine on drift kelp—fronds that have broken off and are making their way to shore. Kelpfish, camouflaged to resemble kelp blades, advance on their prey in wavelike movements, and blood sea stars tiptoe across the sea floor, shedding sperm and eggs from holes between their many arms. On summer evenings like this one, schools of bat rays mate: the male swims under the female, rubbing against her stomach until she accepts him, then they mate in an all-night physical feast, resting during the day. Harbor seals, sea lions, mako, and sand sharks all find refuge in these hundred-and-fifty-foot underwater trees, and the rarely seen giant pelagic jellyfish, with its fifteen-foot-long tentacles, bobs up like the sea's penis, exposing its head to the female envelope of air.

Three hundred thousand million years ago, bits of microcosmic plant life—single cells—began clinging together,

then took purchase on rock. Single-celled plants evolved
into multicelled plants, developing holdfasts, leaves, and bob-
bing gas-filled floats. Finally, the migration from hydrosphere to lithosphere began, and horsetails, fungus, and ferns
gave way to orchids, grasses, flowering shrubs, and majestic
stands of trees that produced fruit, nuts, needles, syrup, and
leaves.

Midnight. I lay out my bedroll on the wheelhouse deck.
Behind red curtains, James, Brendan, Ivan, and Scott play
cards. While we traipsed across the island all day, they went
diving. Their wet suits and spears hang from hooks at my
feet. When the moon rises, James emerges and walks around
to the bow of the boat. He doesn't have to ask if I'm all
right—he can see me smiling. I watch the moon throw his
shadow up; he stands with arms akimbo and one leg bent
back as the *Peace* swings on her anchor.

The Chumash say the moon is a single woman with a
house near the sun. She is called *alahtin,* and Fernando says
she has cleansing powers, that her "forces move the sea,
extend all the way to the stars and control the menses of
women and all creatures, even the oak tree."

Lying on my back, I feel the tide change. Waves travel
as swells, giant ripples that glide toward shore, where they
demolish themselves. If islands have to do with boundaries—
or the loss of them—here, the rind of earth rubs itself down
into water, and water and air become the same thing, always
exchanging chemical and physical balances, like trading
clothes, so that sea and atmosphere are one caldron from
which weather is brewed.

Geophysicists tell me Earth is an island which has two

oceans: the one we are floating on, that thin film clinging to the rocky surface of the planet; the other interior, a molten ball of iron the size of Mars, which forms the earth's core. It is in this hot ocean that inverted mountains of mantle material intrude like upside-down cones.

Now waves roll under the *Peace,* pulled by a Chumash moon. The lights in the wheelhouse have gone out, and the boat rocks from side to side. I can't sleep. The channel's cyclonic eddies spin me, half awake, my feet turning like a clock's second hand. A seal barks. In Wyoming, when a single coyote yips, he is trying to locate himself, to find home. On the water, floating continents of vegetation undulate, and red threads hang down: kelp bed, water home, holdfast deeper than I can see. . . . Will I be cut loose during the night? Will I drift free?

Morning. The engines rev, and we pull out of the harbor. Glancing homeward across the channel, I look for signs of the drought that has embraced California for five years. The Chumash knew periods of drought too. During one, all the streams dried up, the grasses died, and the animals. Even in this abundant paradise, malnutrition appeared. One day a whale beached and died on shore. Runners were sent all over the Chumash nation to tell people that there was food, carrying the sick and elderly on their backs.

The great whale was carved up, meat was distributed, and everyone was fed. During the ceremony held immediately after to thank the gods, it started to rain. Rain continued for weeks and the drought was over. No whale has beached on California shores, and hot winds from the desert blow yellow strings of smog out into the ocean.

In unusually calm waters, the *Peace* glides around the western end of San Miguel. We pass Harris Point, where the Lesters are buried, Wilson's Rock, Richardson's Rock, Castle Rock, and we come to Point Bennet, where three major shipwrecks have occurred. Moving slowly, James eases the *Peace* shoreward. A wonderfully pungent guano smell fills the air, and the beach is covered with sea lions, harbor seals, fur seals, elephant seals—perhaps ten thousand of them—back to back, nose to nose, flipper to flipper, packed together Coney Island style.

During the 1976 Bicentennial, a group of mixed-blood Chumash descendants who called themselves the Brotherhood of the Tomol made a canoe trip to the islands. A waterman and a friend of the tribe, Pete Howorth, helped them build a *tomol* called the *Helek*. "We're urban Indians. We don't know how to do these things," Frank Gutierrez told me. Pete taught them to paddle, then hauled their *tomol* to San Miguel, where the trip would begin. They offered up traditional songs: "Give room. Do not get discouraged. Help me reach the place. Hurrah."

Paddling was difficult. In the choppy passage between San Miguel and Santa Rosa, they almost gave up, then found a way to paddle that worked. "A spirit lifted us up, and we flew across the top of the water," Sespe said. "Five miles went by before we knew it, then the cliffs of the island were above us. When we passed an old Chumash village site, we felt the People watching us."

They suffered sunburn and blisters, ran out of cigarettes, and had a shark scare. "But all the time we were out there, the women at home, our wives, told us they could hear us singing. At night they heard our voices. We may

not have looked like traditional Chumash, but something
was happening, something we can still feel."

Calm seas, clear skies, hot sun. We back out between rocks
and shoals and begin our trip homeward. With wind and
current behind us, the *Peace* surfs forward, almost planing
from the top of one wave to the next. We slide by San
Miguel and Santa Rosa. A Navy "listening station" erected
after World War II to protect the coast from enemy sub-
marines is a white ear on top of Santa Cruz. I stand in front
of the wheelhouse and cup my ears. Diesel engines roar; I
listen for singing.

ARCHITECTURE

*L*ate fall in Wyoming is the end of barefoot days, of nights under single cotton blankets, looking at stars; it is the end of carelessness. "Survive," my body calls out as the first blizzard whips by. No human shelter seems sturdy enough. Why didn't I fly south with my bachelor duck or dig into a steep mountain slope and sleep with the bears? The horses turn tail to oncoming storms and huddle in a clump of cottonwoods. The cattle go down-country, finding shelter in low-spreading junipers.

Walking home from hunting camp last week, my foot fell into a bear track. Not a perfect fit, but my heel pressed

151

into the sow's heelprint as if I were her twin. Her tracks led up a hill into pine trees where I knew from other years, she'd had a den. Bears are particular about their winter quarters. They like a steep slope facing away from prevailing winds, and deep snow, and sometimes an overhanging boulder or log under which to dig. When denning time comes, a bear may travel hundreds of miles to return to a site that stuck in her mind months before as suitable winter quarters. My question is, what is it that brings a bear back? The sound of a waterfall, the scent of whortleberries, the way the breeze brushes her fur coat smooth?

Dens vary, as human houses do. There's an entryway, a long tunnel, sometimes straight, sometimes angled, then one or two sleeping rooms, small enough to trap the bear's body heat, and a sleeping platform laid with the soft tips of pine boughs. The bear smooths the walls with her paws, as if smoothing mortar. Because she bears her young inside the den, she's careful about disclosing her whereabouts. She'll wait to start digging until a good snow begins to fall, filling in her tracks. One biologist saw a bear actually back away from the den using her own tracks so whoever came along would think she was still there. Some sites are hidden, some so spectacularly precarious as to pique our imaginations, such as the den three quarters of the way up an almost vertical wall next to a three-hundred-fifty-foot waterfall.

Orientation, room shape, slope, wind direction, weather: what moves a bear to select a site? Does the idea stay firm in her mind all summer, or year after year? What does the idea look like? Is it a blueprint, a landscape description, a scent? Where in her mind do room designs evolve?

Wyoming has no indigenous architecture, unless it's

the outlaw cave. The log cabin was an idea imported in the 1600s by Swedish immigrants in what is now Delaware, and it moved west along with the settlers. In the mountains I often come on trappers' cabins—tiny structures built close to the ground, with one window and a small door so low even I have to bend over to enter. Homesteaders who arrived just as winter was setting in made do with what they could find: some lived in wall tents or tipis, others in tiny one-room cabins made of logs or adobe, where husband, wife, children, and relatives could only have huddled.

No architectural legacy has taken hold. Housing has a temporary look: sheep wagons, section cars, trailer houses. As one old-timer said, "Everything from the old days has burned down at least once." Here and there are hermits' huts or a basement house whose presence is revealed only by the pickup trucks parked around the roof. New houses built from Boise Cascade kits are perched aboveground and face the highway with an unopenable picture window, so that a passerby can see the cool glow of the television screen at night, but the hermetically sealed residents can't reach out to the world. And throughout the state, there are hundreds of miles where there has never been any human habitation at all.

Warm days return. On the lake at the ranch, ice cracks and thaws in a wavy line across the middle, then a long chunk breaks out like a leg and floats alone in the water as if trying to stand, to make its escape before the arrival of winter. Elsewhere, imbricated plates of ice have thawed and re-frozen and are layered like fish scales, while beneath in the mud, fish and frogs sleep.

Nearby I come on a grackle's nest suspended in the

forked branch of a currant bush. Ingeniously placed, it uses the running water from a ditch as a moat to protect the eggs from ground predators. A nest is a cup of space and represents the transformation of the stochastic natural order to the social one. The sins of human architecture—the ways our houses barricade us from natural forces and all human feeling—send me to the dictionary to look for answers, and I find this: the German word for "building" is derived from a word, *bin,* that also means "to be," and the Japanese for "nest" can be read doubly as "to live."

The house should not be separate, a hollow sculpture conforming to an architect's ego. Rather, it should invoke something of how a human moves and breathes; it should be the flexible casing for metabolism. The first house is the uterus—or else, the neck: in one species of frog, tadpoles incubate in the throat of the father, and when they are big enough, they swim out of his mouth to freedom. All animals are natural builders. Ants of one genus use their bodies architectonically, functioning as both doors and doorkeepers. Flattened in front, with enlarged heads, they fit into the entrance of the anthill with a carpenter's precision. They're color coded to match the soil and savvy enough to allow entrance when secret knocks and smells are emitted.

How desultory most human shelters must seem: all padding and armor, with wall-to-wall carpets, curtains, extraneous decor. I see houses, schools, hospitals built with windows that can't be opened. How can a child understand the rhythms of life if he or she is sealed away from seasons and weather? The new parts of our cities are mirrored and self-referential facades. How can I see into the soul of a building when it has no eyes? Everywhere, unforgiving materials are used, which can't absorb human sweat or hold warmth, or the drumlike beat of sobbing, singing, or laughter. Who wants to make love on the wrong side of mirrored glass?

After breakfast I ride my colt. He is tall and good-looking and likes to put his head down low and set out at a fast walk. Down in the valley, I ride by a field where the shadows of trees have turned white. The rising sun has burned away all the frost on the field except where tree trunks blocked the rays. All that is left are white images of trees lying flat on mown grass—ghostly apparitions—as if matter had borrowed from spirit, and spirit from matter. Later, when I ride home, the frost has melted and the shadows the trees made are black again.

I put my horse away and climb a low knob where I've often thought of building a house. Facing east, I can see up and down this long valley: eleven-thousand-foot peaks to the north, red mesas and another distant mountain range to the south. Directly below my feet, an irrigation ditch curves around the hill like a moat, and beyond are the island and the lake. I sit on a granite boulder sloughed off the face of the mountain who knows how many thousands of years ago. The lichen on its surface is green and black, and the ground is gruss—rotted granite—scoured down into pale red soil.

To start, but how? I think of the Lost Woman of San Nicolas Island, off my hometown in California, who wore cormorant-skin dresses and built a house of whale ribs. The ribs of a horse, cow, or buffalo would make a much smaller house, too small, in fact, but what a wonderful thought: to live in a shelter made from skeletal remains, a body inside a body—but then again, logs and rocks are another kind of bone. Frank Lloyd Wright says: "From nature inward; from within outward." I want to break down the dichotomy between inside and outside, interior and exterior, beauty and ugliness, form and function, because they are all the same.

In a deep bathtub I read about cosmic strings. Dense, invisible, high-energy threads, they unwound from the nuclear explosion at the moment of the Big Bang and function as cosmic two-by-fours, building matter into galactic neighborhoods. But unlike studs, cosmic strings, besides being invisible, are in constant, flexing motion. The physicist Alexander Vilenkin describes them: "Wiggling violently from tension, curved strings often cross themselves and one another. They break at the point of intersection and join again in different configurations. A closed loop splits when it twists on itself. Long coiled strings cross themselves many times over and closed loops get lopped off at intersections." A house is not an empty shell but a path that crosses itself.

It begins to snow. I'm in my own eighty-year-old house, which is uninsulated and made of a poured gypsum block that is crumbling like aspirin. Cold rises through a thin pine floor and pours through the walls. Soon fat flakes will line the arms of trees. All is white except for the thawed circle at the center of the lake, a blowhole through which the planet breathes.

Cosmic strings are flaws that occurred in the featureless vacuum of space; they look like the cracks in lake ice as water freezes, or like fault lines in the earth. From the beginning, the universe was built on symmetries undoing themselves into asymmetries: from the symmetry of featurelessness to the asymmetry of texture and topography. Design is a form of imperfection. It comes from within, it is dictated by the unruliness of nature. A house is bent into shape by space, topography, and prevailing winds; in turn, its captured space reshapes what is beyond its walls.

Another blizzard comes. As I walk, I try to make out which is the lake and which is dry land. Blowing snow "vanishes" me. What I can see is only snow pouring through bronze reeds onto ice like snakes, and as I try to find my way, I think how much a house is like a body, trying to point its feet the right way, trying to see, trying to let in light. House building is a process of locating oneself on the planet, about reading landscape, bending branches down and lifting a structure back up.

When I finally reach the house, I sit on the veranda. Snow stings my face. The walls of traditional Japanese houses open onto verandas that face on gardens, streams, bamboo forests, mountains, or ocean. A house is a platform on which the transaction between nature and culture, internal and external, form and formlessness occurs. Too often "inside" is equated with a static sort of security, a blockade against the commotions of nature, against the plurality of ourselves, while "outside" has come to signify everything that is not human, everything inimical.

A blueprint should be a spiritual proposition: walls and windows become a form of discipline, an obstruction that liberates space and spirit by giving it form. Space is viscous and visceral. It can be held in the hand or in the mind; a body can curve around it, or a room. It starts right here at my lips. I gulp it in, and it oxygenates my blood. I swallow space; I wedge it into my psyche as a way of lifting the roof

of the mind off the noise of thoughts, so that in the inter-
vening silence, any kind of willful spirit can express itself.

I come up with this: If I built a house, a stream would
trickle through the main room, then continue on, threading
together gardens, studies, bathrooms. A rock wall made
from the granite strewn across the house site would bolster
the house against prevailing northwesterly winds. A dense
forest of bamboo or aspen would frame the twisted entrance,
thinning out until it opened into a room. Walls, ceilings,
floors jutting out beyond sliding doors, would be made of
local materials: cottonwood, pine, fir, granite, willow
branches braided with sage. Floor levels would change with
topography, function, view, the way the basins of waterfalls
do, catching pools of activity, then spilling them again.
Rooms would not have common walls. Covered verandas
or corridors would link bedrooms, bathrooms, studies, and
on the way, an alcove might invite the passerby in to sit and
look at a hill where swifts and swallows nest, or open onto
a tiny garden. Passageways would lift me up or down, alter
my pace, my sense of self. A granite boulder would burst
through the wall of the main room to remind me that a
wall, like a thought, is a flexible thing, that a house is not
a defense *against* nature but a way of letting it in. In the
kitchen, polished granite slabs would serve as counters. I
might spread gruss under my feet near south-facing windows to absorb heat; I might have trees growing next to
books. I'd let fault lines tell me where to elevate or drop a
floor; clouds might shape the ceiling. The way the house
moved over the contour of the land would be the way it
speaks.

. . .

I'm on the knob again. The sun is out, and the hole in the center of the lake has thawed, though I don't know yet that this is the last time I'll see open water. If only my bachelor duck could see the lake's opening, would he return? At dusk the hole is a pot of gold-gilded ripples, a way of looking into the earth's belly, but in the morning winter sets in.

It snows: six inches, then seven more, until the white is continuous, day and night, lifting the level of the ground twenty, thirty, forty inches. The wind howls, and during interstices coyotes howl back. The light is flat, and the land-scape is ever-changing: drifts curve down from buildings and fence lines; sagebrush, fence lines, roadbeds, and five-strand barb-wire fences have all disappeared.

How far away autumn seems now, and its many days of burnished ruddiness. Like a house built into a hill, winter is cantilevered over all that. I can no longer see the lake, distinguish the knob from the flat, though the lake ice groans, shifting under the muffle of snow. An Alaskan bi-ologist who lives on pack ice at Resolute Bay and in the Chukchi and Beaufort seas four months of the year says, "Reading the landscape up there means watching a whole topography come into existence. Ice collides and forms pres-sure ridges. I watch entire mountains come into existence. And just when I'm getting to know my way around in this newly formed landscape, the ice melts, the formations are gone, and my intimacy with that place is over."

Matsuo Bashō writes, in the essay "Hut of the Phantom Dwelling": "The grebe attaches its floating nest to a single strand of reed, counting on the reed to keep it from washing away in the current." By what thin strands of luck we stay alive and know in which direction our feet are pointing!

The snow continues. I keep thinking of the Crow word for loneliness, which translates literally as "I can't see myself." Perhaps the word was composed during a blizzard. Every morning my husband harnesses his team of black Percherons, and we make our way down what appears to have been a road—now mounded with drifts—to feed the cows. It's a twelve-mile round trip. The dogs, running ahead, vanish under the snow, then leap straight up into the air as if to say, "I'm still here."

Wind has carved the landscape into an impenetrable being, and worked snow down steep slopes into white whorls of brocade. When the storm ends, the sky clears fast, and at night it is thirty below zero. In the morning, sun hits the top of the mountain: light moving down the slope looks like cream being poured.

Winter solstice. How quickly the sun flies across the southern sky, ringed by a huge halo: a sun dog. At night constellations are blueprints, pointing the way between twists of cosmic strings. The winter night I flew out of Fairbanks, Alaska, a folding curtain of northern lights pulsed upward and pierced the Big Dipper, as if trying to follow an architect's plan, trying to unfold itself into rooms.

THE FASTING HEART

February 28. Again and again winter's brightness reveals possibilities, yet I drive its cold spine
into my back and lose all feeling. In December I watched
the sun lower itself to the horizon and saw how snowbanks
rose up to it like a wave far out at sea, growing bigger as
it pushed for shore. A shadow passes over the place where
I know the lake to be; the lake is a white flat, featureless,
with fenders of snow bending up into the night. Above me,
mountains walk in clouds, are made of clouds. Beneath,
hidden lake ice moans: *Oh, darling, what are you saying
to me?*

The fasting heart knows hunger but is denied. It breaks and is set wrong: the leg that walks crooked must be broken again to go straight. Emptiness fills the heart until it bursts, and the salt water pouring out is a cord on which disparate elements are a ribbon of chaos.

Looking around, I see presages of spring. Willow branches are bumpy with tight buds, and melting flecks of frost in dirt are lights going out. Yet more snow comes, deep and soft. On the mountain there are tracks made by elk, narrow trails pounded deep into scree. I ski to the gate at the top of one mountain—a gate that leads nowhere—and remember how in spring wind swings it open and closed as if all snow came onto the earth this way and by the same route was fanned away.

Lately I've had to redefine the word "knowledge" to a knowledge that cannot know anything. I'm dealing not in careless absurdities here but in the way material reality is unobservable and implicit order can be found in paradox. Perhaps despair is the only human sin. Who am I to feel disappointment? Is a bird disappointed in the sky? I read Lao Tzu: "Concentrate your will. Hear not with your ears but with your mind; not with your mind but with your spirit. Let your hearing stop with the ears, and let your mind stop with its images. Let your spirit, however, be like a blank, passively responsive to externals. In such open receptivity only can Tao abide. And that open receptivity is the fasting of the heart."

To fast does not mean to go without but to become empty and in so doing open oneself. I am at the beginning of a new month, and spring is here. Snow comes when there is sun; sun shines, but I can see my breath. When the shadow finally slides from the hidden lake, I try not to long for open water but to see how light and darkness makes sense of these days, how it separates planes of thought and gives distinction to landscape.

I spend the night on my tiny island, Alcatraz, and watch the morning star and the dark side of the planet go bright. Then a light snow falls and steam from the earth rises into it, coming back down as a shroud. It was on an island in the North Sea that Werner Heisenberg, recovering from a bout of hay fever, formulated the first quantum theory. Strolling those desolate northern beaches, he recalled his conversations in student days with Niels Bohr and understood that the world, in all its diversity, is made of a single substance: quantum stuff, whose variety is manifested not as substance but as process, not in palpable form but in the way it moves.

It's March. I don't know the date. Tonight during a full moon, I watch a bank of clouds break off from a mountaintop and feel something break in me. Each thought brings forth a new world, and in this way, consciousness creates experience. Thoughts walk, new worlds are lost, and the losing brings forth another ephemeral continent, motion giving birth to motion.

In the morning I walk to the falls, taking notes on the erotic positions of winter-killed deer. "Even in death . . . ," my journal begins, though it is not about sex that I write but about how the body itself is a complete truth. Why, then, does life seem embellished with sadness? I fight against the optical illusion of separateness. Quantum physics tells me the experience of isolation is a fantasy, that I am part of a whole. Yet my heart literally hurts, saying these things.

Mid-March. From now on all my journal entries read: 2:00 A.M. It's calving time, and I'm on the night shift, which means checking heifers and older cows every two hours from 11:00 P.M. until six in the morning. When the snow is deep, I ski between sleeping animals, who no longer pay attention to my strange gear. Tonight no calves come. Just before the sky lightens, a breeze picks up as if wind were clearing the palate of bad dreams, the difficulties of birth and living.

Days, I take wolf naps, lying on the ground with pregnant cows, the small bodies inside already unfolding, swimming in liquid, pawing with tiny hooves to get out. Their symphony of cud chewing, gurgling bellies, grunts and belches, teeth grinding, lulls me, and as I call to them by name, they respond, sweet-eyed, diffident, and calm.

Down the line of hay I notice a cow beginning to give birth. Two front feet appear through the drapery of a broken water bag. Unbothered, the cow keeps eating. As labor increases, she finally lies down and pushes hard. Within minutes, the head emerges, floppy-eared and wet, then the hips and back legs. The cow gets up, and I watch her look of irritation and bewilderment change to a wild, giddy sweetness as she licks and nudges, making gentle lowing sounds, welcoming her new calf into the world.

Morning. A waterspout of mist blows straight up from behind a ridge and wafts against eight thousand vertical feet of granite. Spring fountains life onto the earth this way, pumping warm air into Arctic nights and new calves onto the ground. Usually it's snow and deep cold we have to contend with, but this week it's a sudden thaw, which brought disaster when the temperature rose from twenty below zero to sixty above in twelve hours, melting the three feet of snow that had lain on the ground all winter. At dawn there is water running everywhere. Rivers flood pastures. I find calves with only their heads above water and do my best to get them to high ground. It takes one teaspoon of bacteria to infect a thousand cows; we have many less than that, and by midday bacterial and viral scours, plus quick pneumonia, are rampant. Some calves become so sick they lie flat on the ground, their mouths cold, tongues hanging out, dying from dehydration. A friend, Erv, comes to help. Together we take temperatures, give shots and boluses, tube and bottle-feed calves with our vet's recommended home remedy: warmed-up beef consommé. Erv holds the calf upright between his knees, and I give the bottle, working the jaw to stimulate a sucking motion.

Doctoring sick calves becomes my sole work. I don't even notice when or where the new ones were born. My days and nights are lived in the herd, and an intimacy blossoms as it does when one attends any gravely ill being, after talk becomes impossible or unnecessary to exchange.

One night the temperature drops to twenty below, and just at dark I notice a yearling steer has broken through lake ice and is half submerged. We drive the pickup to the edge, rope his horns, dally to the trailer hitch, and pull him slowly out. In the squeeze chute, I dry him with a tiny hair dryer, then put him to bed in a shed piled with fresh straw. By morning he is healthy, but more calves are dead.

Every few days a blizzard whips up fast—from clear

sky to whiteout in fifteen minutes—and we try to move the newborn calves and their mothers to sunsheds so they won't freeze to the ground or suffocate in drifting snow. After one such move, a calf is missing. I hike back up to the pasture above the house. Up there the wind is blowing so hard I am bent double. On hands and knees, I search under giant sagebrush for the animal. Nothing. Then out across the flat I see something moving: the calf is being blown across the ground. Running, I tackle him, and for a while we lie huddled together.

It's said that enlightenment is trackless, that the path of knowledge and the path of ignorance are the same. Snow covers us. There is no telling how we got there, where we could go. All I know is this: I am the calf's anchor in a storm, and he, mine. Unseeing, unmoving, which path am I on?

The end of March. Where is spring? Rain is followed by snow which is followed by rain. Snow on shed roofs loosens and slides, lying broken and glistening on the ground in huge crystals. A flock of finches descends from a passing cloud, bringing song to the earth for the first time since fall. Snow on the lake curdles, and underneath, the ice cover has grayed like bruised skin. Sun shifts its long-legged rays through clouds walking across seasons. Mist dissolves in juniper fronds. Wind deepens: winter is so difficult to dislodge. I hear it groan as it leaves: *Oh, darling, why are you doing this to me?*

I think of the night when I stayed at the house of the novelist Osamu Dazai in northern Japan, now an inn. I couldn't sleep. It had been raining on and off, but there was a full moon. I slipped out of my Meiji-era, second-story, foreign-style room, with its high ceilings and French doors, and walked the narrow hallways of the otherwise traditional Japanese house. Under my feet floorboards chirped—what Japanese call "nightingale floors"—and wind rattled long horizontal windows. I looked down at the heaving shoulders of a tree in the courtyard and thought of the Japanese pivot word *nagame,* used in poems to mean, simultaneously: "long rains," "reverie," "thinking of love."

At dinner I had met a young Japanese man. With his angular nose and sensuous lips, he looked princely, but his hands shook as he brought the sake cup to his mouth, and his face reddened after it was suggested by the proprietress that he and I should become friends. It's stylish now in Japan to drink coffee instead of tea, so following custom, I sat in the tiny lobby sipping espresso and thumbing through one of Dazai's novels, *The Setting Sun.* Glancing around once, I found the young man sitting opposite, staring at me.

Late that night, sleepless and walking the halls, I came on his room. The sliding door was partway open. The storm had broken, and moonlight shone in on his perfect face. I could see his hands clasped together and the sleeves of his indigo *yukata* folded in triangles across his chest. Was he asleep or awake? Why was his door open?

Wind battered the house. In Dazai's novel he wrote: "Last night we drank together and I put her to bed in the foreign-style room on the second floor. I laid out bedding for myself in the room downstairs where Mama died. Then I began to write this wretched memoir. Kazuko, I have no room for hope. Good-bye." After which, in real life, he and his lover gave their lives in a double suicide.

Book in hand, I stood in this stranger's doorway watching moonlight shake across his face. I listened. Would he call out for me? His breathing was deep and slow. Whispering, I said good-night.

April 1. Open water. Hot days, seventy degrees, and the hard, monastic rules of dormancy are finally broken. The world repopulates itself with ducks. Pairs of mallards crowd in at the warm end of the lake, feeding on watercress, bugs, and aquatic weeds. Then goldeneyes, terns, avocets, coots, godwits, wigeons, and phalaropes fly in from points south, guided by moonlight and stars and magnetic fields. A secret organ inside their chests helps them detect compass points, and as they glide in for landings on the water, I wonder if we too have a place in our bodies that guides us.

I sleep on the island in the pond. During the night more birds arrive. Humpbacked, the island bends me, thrusting my pelvis. "These yearnings, what are they?" the poet Walt Whitman asked. Mallards fly at night, navigating by their internal compass as well as by the position of moon and stars. What is it that magnetizes me to one person, one landscape, then another? Seemingly stationary, I attempt to locate myself, knowing that when I look at the Milky Way, I am looking laterally through the galactic equator; that this is just one galaxy—*gala,* from the Greek for "milk"— around which there is a celestial landscape wilder and more turbulent than anything I can imagine or see.

In the dark I look between stars at luminous debris— the building blocks of our solar system—and strain to see where the Oort cloud might be, the birthplace of comets captured by gravitational perturbations and spewed into our local sky like seed.

In 1986 I flew to the big island of Hawaii to observe Comet Halley from NASA's infrared telescope on Mauna Kea. For five hours, the choppy sea below had looked like a field of stars. Ahead, Mauna Kea loomed, snow-covered, nearly 14,000 feet straight out of the sea. A dormant shield volcano, it has long slopes covered with reddish-black lava, which has pooled and hardened on the outskirts of Hilo. The mountain is the sacred home to Pali, whom legend describes as having a mane of black hair, a back straight as a cliff, and breasts rounded like moons.

At the airport I'm met by Roger Kanacke, an astronomer, and his assistant, Tim, and together we drive up through lava fields to Hale Pohaku, or "midlevel," as they call it, a place built for observing astronomers to stay and get acclimatized at 10,000 feet before going up to 13,500 feet, where the observatories are.

Roger is the son of an engineer who designed the parachute for the Apollo mission. When he was ten, his mother gave him a young astronomer's kit—a starfinder and telescope—and after, he knew what he wanted to do with his life. "Astronomers get just as excited about seeing the stars in the night sky as anyone," Roger says, "but now we spend most of our time in windowless rooms with computers. I'm beginning to forget where the stars are."

In the late afternoon we drive to the top of Mauna Kea. At dusk the shadow of the earth rests against a bank of clouds, then a full moon rises, erasing us. Later the moon goes into eclipse, and as the sky darkens, the gauzy tail of Comet Halley appears.

"We are trying to understand the universe from the inside out—it's not even clear if this is possible, because we're part of what we're studying. But we keep pushing what we know back to the tiniest fraction of time, to the moment of the creation of the universe. We are asking the fundamental questions, but I do not know if the answers are forthcoming."

Inside the observatory the infrared telescope seems huge, and at an altitude of almost 14,000 feet, I grow dizzy as I tip my head back to take in the whole machine. There are oxygen tanks on wheels nearby for fainting astronomers. Through a heavy door, we enter the computer room.

At 6:00 P.M. Roger calls the Jet Propulsion Lab in Pasadena, California, to get the coordinates for Comet Halley—where, exactly, in the sky the comet will be—then the telescope operator, a loose-jointed, laid-back young guy from Kona, punches the numbers into the computer. "Gone are the bone-chilling nights standing on a ladder with your eyebrows frozen to the telescope's eyepiece," Roger says, adjusting dials and refiguring equations on a calculator with symbols I've never seen before. Using the intercom, Roger logs in with the telescope operator: Adjust focus. Adjust chopper. Set crosshairs. Focus at 1.5, aperture at 5 mm. "We're going to set up on a bright star," he explains. Then a voice comes over the intercom: "Wind's coming up. It's twenty-five mph now." Roger groans. At forty or fifty miles per hour, the observatories have to shut down.

Luckily, tonight the wind dies. "It takes years to get observing time at these world-class telescopes," Tim explains. "Sometimes we go halfway around the world to observe, then some little thing like the wind shuts us down and we go home having accomplished nothing."

"What star are we on?" Roger asks. "SJ 9523," Tim

replies. "Do we have the Halley coordinates?" "Yes." "Then let 'er rip," Roger says, and a curved door in the ceiling of the dome opens slowly onto the universe.

The core of a comet is made of remnant materials from very early times. Its coma (tail) is a spherical cloud of ice and dust—debris left over from the time of planet building. To see into this sphere is to have a window into the beginnings of time. On the computer screen, Comet Halley appears as a white dot, that's all. During the night there are long periods when nothing seems to happen. Tim reads Dante, Roger falls asleep and jerks awake. Then he turns to me and says: "It must seem strange to you to find out that I spend my life studying dust. If only I could get a handful of it . . . Maybe then I would know something."

Sometime after midnight a "bump" appears in the spectra. It is explained to me as dark material—probably carbon—not seen before. Roger calls Tom Gerballe, an astronomer in one of the other observatories on the mountain. "Did you see it?" Roger asks. "Yes. And they saw it other places too." Roger and I drive to Tom's building. Inside, the atmosphere is markedly different: bright lights, rock music blaring, Tom on his hands and knees in a continuous sea of paper running out of the printer. "Look, it's here and here and here," he yells excitedly, and I see bumps in the masses of wavy lines but fail to understand what the finding means in terms of the comet.

"Is it gas?" "It can't be gas." "Which gas?" "Is it hotter? This doesn't look like any other spectra I've ever seen." "Maybe we'll learn something about comets tonight. . . . Ah, the sky is full of mystery. . . ."

Finally, Tom sits in a chair with an armful of uncut computer printouts. He has slate-blue eyes and wild corkscrew black hair and wears sandals despite deep snow outside. "I just came up here to test an instrument. It's usually so boring—no romance in all this, you know—but now we've made a discovery, even if we don't know what it is we've discovered," he says, laughing. He watches more paper undulate across the floor. "The first night I went to observe as a student, I left home in the fog, drove up the mountain in the fog, unloaded the equipment in the fog, sat all night in the fog. In the morning, I went home in the fog and never knew where I was, which direction I was facing. That's kind of how astronomy is, even on nights like this."

Back at the NASA observatory, Roger, Tim, and I gather the data. "Now the fun begins," Roger says sleepily. "We go home and try to figure this stuff out." Down the treacherous road to Hale Pohaku, I talk nonstop to keep Roger awake at the wheel. Light comes into the sky, and far below, a thick bank of fog carpets the entire island.

"I was born not knowing and have only had a little time to change that here and there," Richard Feynman, the physicist, said. Today I was taken to see a tree. It's April 15, and I'm in north Florida. What Floridians call a "scrub," Wyomingites would call a forest. My guide leads me through pines, palms, and cypress trees. Against a red sky, palmettos hold up their fringed fans, wild vines cling tightly to tree trunks, and the coarse fibers of an uprooted palm are like hair. The trail through a dense thicket stops, and there is an opening. In the distance, a lake spreads before me, gold in morning light.

Florida is a flat limestone shelf that sticks out into the sea. It is all water, runneled through soft rock, breaking open here and there, and whole lakes have been known to drain overnight. But this one shimmers, almost overfull. The slap of alligator tails announces our arrival. Egrets and herons poke around in mud flats, and tall palms at the edge of the water sway as though fanning away the heat to come.

The guide takes me deeper into the woods. Spiderwebs span trees, wrap around my wrists and neck, and ticks fall into my shirt. The spongy ground takes my tracks and lays them onto those of a deer.

In many early cultures, trees, like mountains, were thought to be the axial center of the universe, soaring as they do above human entanglements. It wasn't the tree I saw first but the clearing beneath it: dappled with sunlight, it seemed altarlike, as if we were meant to kneel there. The tree is a live oak soaring straight like a mast but thick as ten masts lashed together. Far up, branches hold moss from their arms as if weighing stories for truths, balancing every disparity in their elegant, judicial spread. Cheek against bark, I look past leaves into the becalmed eye of a Florida morning: "Quercus." Oak. That's the tree's Latin name. It sounds like a question.

Later. Dreamed I held a comet's tail like a tree trunk and carried it to my astronomer friend to look at and explain to me. "Have you ever touched time?" he asked. "No," I said. Then Roger took my hand and put it on a place where pieces of ice and bits of stars bubbled out from a vent in emptiness like the ones at the bottom of the ocean where warm, juvenile water gurgles into being.

Now I'm on water for an afternoon, on the warm gulf

stream, which has been known to carry the seeds of tropical plants as far north as Ireland. Days when sky and sea are the same color, I understand how water currents are stirred by air currents and air currents heated or cooled by water, both functioning as one organism, how it is not correspondence but coherence that matters, that if we do not start with wholeness and unity, we will not end there either.

I read about galactic plasma and marine plasma and the chemical architecture of the human brain. Are the icy contents of a comet's tail—its plasma—red, crystallized blood? The microscopic bits of life floating in a primeval ocean three hundred thousand million years ago marched from hydrosphere to lithosphere, took purchase on rock, plumbed itself, rose up, bearing seed, flower, and fruit, high into the air.

A tree represents the zenith of botanical evolution, it is an aerial garden, far from its oceanic beginnings. A tree is a thought, an obstruction stopping the flow of wind and light, trapping water, housing insects, birds, and animals, and breathing in and out. How treelike the human, how human the tree. It is a thumb held up or a leg striding, the kind of obstacle that causes human and botanical consciousness to occur.

Even the words used to describe the human brain are botanical: limbus—referring to the limbic system, where all emotion occurs—is a word whose ancient meaning was "limb of a tree." Cortex, that deep part of the brain where language and abstract thought happen, means "bark."

I am told of the delicate nature of the tree's parts: of cambium, the inner layer of cells between phloem and xylem, and how remarkably sensitive it is to any strain on the tree.

And the way bark acts as a waterproof covering to the thin layer of living tissue within. A tree's breathing is slow and slight. The respiratory pores in the bark, called lenticels, must have ample space. As the tree ages, the central heartwood thickens and the girth of the trunk widens to accommodate decay.

Gary Lynch, a neurobiologist, has put together the physiology of memory, the way we know what we know. Thoughts arise as electrical impulses; bits of thought and sensation are neural plasma shuttling from cell to cell, spreading like a net. There's a rhythmical pattern of firing activity, and wild chemical reactions occur: calcium is released and in turn activates an enzyme called calpain, which scrubs connective tissue between neurons—the rootlike dendrites—cutting into the cytoskeleton and, in this way, exposing receptors. Through these, information is absorbed; memory is etched in, and the dendritic brainscape, a place that looks like the cracks in ice on my lake, changes its shape forever.

To know something, then, we must be scrubbed raw, the fasting heart exposed.

Wyoming. I wait for light, and when it comes the lake is mine again. It is a black shield, a silver mirror, a black cloth wound around glinting mountains. Ducks waddle on a free-floating piece of ice that bumps into the island. Golden eagles colonize the sky. One area of open water in the lake is shaped like a violin. Wind plays water pizzicato, à la Bartok, plucking strings. At the shallow end, gray mud flats are marked with holes where snipes have thrust their sensitive bills for food. By the end of the week, sun has shrunken lake ice to the size of a dime.

On the evening news Carl Sagan talks about the photographs from the Voyager. He sounds distraught: "There doesn't seem to be any life out there," he reports, "which underscores the rarity and preciousness of life here." One photograph has moved him. It looks back at the earth from the edge of the galaxy. "We look like a blue dot. A blue dot . . . that's all we are."

At dusk I gaze across the lake. My little island, Alcatraz, is a floating hyacinth in rising water, dragging willow branches like oars. Purple swallows dive down for mosquitoes, and the iridescent heads of mallards flash back and forth. Inside a nest hung by pink straps made from willow bark, I see a blue dot—a universe within a universe: the blue egg of a robin.

April 20. White Sands Missile Range, New Mexico. Here I am at ground zero, my fingers stuck through the chain-link fence that surrounds Trinity Site, where the first atomic bomb was detonated on July 16, 1945. This place stands for what could be the end of all life, yet spring is in full bloom and I'm here with the botanist and writer Gary Nabhan, looking for an uncommon cactus, *Toumeya papyracantha,* which survives by giving up its best defense: sharp spines. Also called grama grass cactus or papery spine cactus, it has soft and elongated spines, a camouflage to make it look like the grama grass in whose midst it grows. Red-tailed B-17s fly hot missions over us, low and fast, dropping bombs near Stallion's Gate to the north as we crawl over radioactive ground.

"It took a year to get permission to come onto this land," Gary yells over the roar of bombers. At the main gate we were fingerprinted, photographed, given badges, and sent off with an Army biologist named Kim.

"Don't touch any ordnance," she warns as we search fairy rings of grama grass for the cactus. We are in the supersecret zone where laser explosives are set off to duplicate nuclear detonations and Patriot missiles are fired. Everywhere, pieces and parts of bombs, shells, nose cones, and airplanes stick out of the sand. "Some things might still be hot," Kim says. "You know, unexploded." I keep expecting to find grotesquely enlarged plant specimens, but everything looks quite normal. At my elbow, a phosphorescent beetle with a turquoise back crawls over an unexploded shell, then makes tracks away from me in the sand.

Semis go by with full-grown pine trees, held upright in giant Christmas tree stands. The Army is the greatest producer of theater. "What are they doing?" we ask. "They're making a simulated forest to practice night bombing raids," we are told. A turkey vulture circles us, and an oryx—imported from Africa for fat-cat officers to hunt—looks on as we begin to find and flag toumeya. Looking down into a clump of grama grass, we find it almost impossible to see the cactus, whose papery spines flow out like blond hair. Conformity and camouflage are two ways plants and humans can get along in the world; they can also be a way to hide the means of war. To live in conflict and harmony . . .

In the morning we are barred entry to the missile range. During the night they bombed the "forest," and now they are shooting off missiles that land where, yesterday, we found cactus, so we retreat to nonmilitary lands. A skiff of new snow shines on Sierra Blanca Peak to the north, and to the south, a blimplike object is suspended in the sky, which I'm told is the border patrol's "look-down radar" for drug detection. As we set up ten-by-ten-foot transects where toumeya is particularly thick, a mockingbird mimics the sound of a phone ringing, then a bomber zooming overhead.

We stop to look at a king-sized yucca tree. One species of moth lays its eggs inside the ovary of the yucca flower, showering pollen onto the stigma as it does so, inadvertently pollinating the plant. When the eggs develop, the larvae feed on yucca seeds, leaving enough for the plant to reseed itself . . . a classic example of botanical love: the plant unable to live without the animal, and vice versa.

On another road we examine a buffalo gourd, so precisely adapted to the desert's short rainy season that it can emerge from dormancy to flower in just twenty days. The plant is pollinated by an unusual bee whose body is shaped perfectly to fit inside the male flower. The bee goes there to sleep at night and backs out at dawn, carrying pollen grains on its back as it visits the female flower.

Two by two, F-15s make their morning assaults on my ears as I crawl on hands and knees through stands of cactus endangered by its defenselessness and think how cooperation and competition can be the same thing, two sides of the same coin. At midmorning I find a robust, two-headed toumeya, the biggest one so far. Head propped on my hand, I memorize the cactus's form and shape and listen to the mockingbird sing obsessively—one song after another—and wonder what makes any song one's own. Then it occurs to me that this cactus's best defense is a peaceful one: not meting out pain but merely blending in.

Conclusions end in new questions. Why would a cactus live in the middle of grasses that are routinely grazed? Have I missed the obvious? Perhaps the point is to be eaten, so the ingested seeds can be distributed through the manure of the grazing animal. The lesson here is implicit: some things die in order to survive: individual sacrifice for the greater, common good. But isn't that what they tell young soldiers going to war?

More F-15s streak by, and another mock forest has been created and destroyed. Here, on the missile range, death is thought to have the power to end things. But that truth is incomplete. There is also this: the origin of life is always found in death; death is life's constant companion.

Home again. It's almost May, and I climb the dry bed of Cedar Creek, looking for meltwater. Scrambling up boulders, down steep sides, over fallen trees, I finally come to a grotto. Pine wind drives into it, scouring its walls as though readying it for spring. Bird song reports against red walls in sharp echoes. Looking upcanyon, I see towering peaks trimmed in snow—our storehouse of water.

At the mouth of the grotto I touch my toe to a pool covered with ice—delicate as eggshell, it splinters. I dreamed last night of three waterfalls whose flow had been transfixed as crystal bowls that wouldn't stop breaking; then, falling, they became whole again. A long icicle at the front of the cave drips—the tick of a heart.

The word "grotto" comes in a roundabout way from *crypta,* meaning "hidden" or "to hide," and is related to an old Norse word that means "pile of stones." Two huge, whalelike boulders lean out from the gorge, cantilevered over my head, and where they split apart is wedged a single, egg-shaped rock, glazed over with ice—a transparent cocoon inside of which stirs an unborn being: a bug, a whale, a bird.

We turn our cattle out onto the range. Thousands of acres are split into temporary hundred-acre pastures by the use of electric fences, and we move the cattle, sheep, and one guard donkey through these quickly—depending on the growth rate of the grass, it's about every three days—in order to avoid overgrazing and damage to the whole ecosystem. Short-duration, high-intensity grazing duplicates the movement of buffalo pursued by predators (human and animal) over these lands. For protection they bunched up, trampled ground, grazed, then quickly moved on. In this way, few, if any, grass plants were bitten off more than once.

Now I'm on my hands and knees again, regarding a blade of grass, not only to see myself in it, as Whitman did, but to understand what a grass plant needs to flourish. It should be grazed once, and the root systems left to restore themselves; it needs to be fertilized by the animals who use it and watered by rains.

In Japan I visited the Taoist farmer Masanobu Fukuoka, who said, "In order to restore the balance of the natural world, we have to change our attitudes. We have to learn to do less. People plant with their heads. They think they have to do many things, but they are wrong. It's the *kamisama* who do the growing; we just help out a little bit. We must stop thinking we know anything. Better to take our clothes off and roll around on the ground like babies. We have to give up everything before we can begin."

As we walked to his hillside farm, bird song erupted

and a wild tangle of vegetation took over from neatly pruned farms below. Cucumber vines climbed persimmon trees; peaches dropped into winter gardens of scallions, cabbage, daikon. Narcissus bloomed around mandarin orange trees whose unpicked fruit was split open and eaten by birds. "If they like it, it must be good," Fukuoka exclaimed happily. He grows rice as it's meant to be grown—like any wild grain, started from seed, sprouting in soil, not water. "Why do people think they have to plant rice any other way? They must be crazy! So much work. The *kamisama* laugh at us. Really, things are very simple."

I try to cultivate my thinking and manage the land for biodiversity. Let one good thing happen, and there are many results. Stop overgrazing, and more plants—grasses, wildflowers, shrubs, trees—cover the ground and more species occur. As a result there are more bugs, more birds, more small and large animals, a better energy and mineral cycle. Intermittent streams begin to flow year round. In a few years' time there is more of everything, and these open spaces begin to fill with life.

May. High water. One stream comes down, then another, until meltwater pours from every direction onto the ranch. There are creeks where none existed before, and the front yard is a wide pool buzzing with mosquitoes. Bird song rolls over tumbling cataracts, falling into the catcher's mitt of the human ear. Snow is gone. If snow represents renunciation, then I renounce renunciation. By afternoon a snake dance of red silt stains running water, and drinking it, I feel red threads pull through me, the red threads of desire.

Mornings and evenings I irrigate a hundred acres, setting dams in ditches to stop the flow of the creek and divert
it onto fields of native hay. Standing knee-deep in water, I
recklessly declare this to be the end of the drought. Fields
that have been dry for three years are inundated, water
working its way around hard stems like an embrace. How
good it must feel to drink with the whole body. At the end
of the day a bird, hidden from sight, sings a song I've never
heard before.

A front comes in. I ride to the mountaintop gate—the
gate that leads nowhere—and watch shifting mists hide
running herds of elk. Truncated rainbows stab the green
slope; rain comes as an act of generosity, as if the sky's big
body had pulled itself apart for me to see.

I go back to the grotto on Cedar Creek. Moss climbs
the walls, and little ferns poised on rock ledges receive spray.
Way back in the crypt, a pool has formed, and water dripping out of a seam in the rocks feeds it continuously. I walk
through the waterfall—hair and clothes drenched—and, on
the other side, crouch down under sloping walls. Shoes off,
I put my toe into the pool: silt rises in plumes, hiding me.

"Passion too deep seems like none," a Chinese Tang poet
wrote. Walking down the mountain from Cedar Creek, I
think of Raku-san, the fifteenth-generation potter I visited
whose family's hot firing technique has made their ware
famous around the world. Steeped in a thousand years of
pottery-making tradition, he lives by breaking with that
tradition. At his house in Kyoto we were led into a cold,
empty reception room and sat "women's style"—on our
knees. After a long wait, Raku-san's wife appeared dressed
in a black leather miniskirt, and served us sweets and tea

ceremony tea. Then Raku-san burst in. Tall, graceful, handsome, he had an easy laugh he claimed to have acquired while living in Rome during the sixties. He was dressed in formal priest's attire, since he was only taking a break from performing the tea ceremony at a nearby temple as part of the New Year's celebration. "The formal duties of the eldest son of such a family of National Living Treasures are worse than those of royalty," my friend and interpreter Leila said, "because royalty aren't expected to make art too."

After we talked, he asked us if we would like to see some of his new work. No one else in Japan had had this privilege, we found out later. He set four tea bowls in front of us on the tatami. They were unlike any others I have seen: oversized, oddly shaped, marked boldly with grays, greens, oozing red glaze. "Each tea bowl is a canvas," Leila said, holding one. I tried to register the feel of another bowl in my hand: smooth and bumpy, delicate and heavy. Sitting cross-legged, leaning one elbow on a knee, then the other, Raku-san watched us, smiling. His hands and arms were muscular and heavily veined, and all the beauty of his bowls shone in his face—the one lighting up the other.

"My bowls have caused some controversy," he said. "They aren't appropriate for traditional tearooms now. So I've decided to design a new kind of tearoom to match my bowls. They'll be bigger and a little wilder. . . ." He talked about the house he is building in the mountains outside Kyoto and the place where he digs clay—the same place his grandfather dug his and where Raku-san's grandchildren will dig theirs. "Sometimes I feel something over my shoulder like a ghost," he said. "It scares me a little bit, but it's just my grandfather telling me what to do."

"Does your grandfather tell you to make your tea bowls

like these—wild and passionate and free?" I asked him. A faint smile came over his face: "Yes."

Later in the day I decided to make my own ink. I boiled bones, twigs, bark, and added powders bought in Kyoto: vermilion, cerulean, purple, green mixed with dried deer hooves. The colored liquid resulting from my brew was brackish and faded when I wrote. John Muir more successfully made ink from his beloved sequoia trees, and Ikkyū, the Japanese poet-monk, abbot of Daitoko-ji, favored the charcoal of orchid trees for his. Another monk made white ink from cuttlefish bones and called it "the ten-thousand-times-pounded frost flower," commenting also that "as ink is made through many poundings, so too the spirit suffers ordeals."

June. Flowers from the apple tree fall, and I feel the bulbs at the end of branches swelling into fruit. Clouds of yellow pine pollen billow past. Now the gate on the mountaintop is sun-whitened against a black sky, and the island in the lake is a brain studying itself, not only remembering remembering but knowing how the remembering takes place. Receptors exposed, everything ordinary turns into an exotic aperçu.

I saddle my young horse, ride out into a field, and ask him to stand quietly. This he will not do. Instead we take the pilgrim's loop: from lake to grotto, grotto to tablets, tablets to lake. Now the gate that leads nowhere is black, and the mountains behind it are white with unseasonal snow. When we trot home, a cloud throws huge hailstones like miniature comets to the ground, as if my uncertainty had become a form of gravitational pull.

The fasting heart slides from extreme to extreme, looking for quiescence, longing for longing to be assuaged. To fast means to put nothing in the body. It also means leaving nothing out. Is that why I keep breaking into myself like a thief, not stealing but filling up on hope and fear? Borrowing a stethoscope from the vet's kit, I listen to my own heart. Its beats are slow and fast, sure and unsure, arrhythmical and steady-state. Again and again, during the long summer, it is knocked open by a flicker's drumming love tap, and the skin that covers tissue is pecked away.

Sometimes I wonder if the fasting heart is not another term for gluttony. At dawn in a friend's hillside house, I hear a grove of bamboo rustle, and from it the world's smallest bird, the hummingbird, flies into the room, spinning around and around as if trying to show me how to draw the outlines of self bigger. What I'm talking about is not illusions of grandeur but how, in emptiness, I could become more inclusive, evolving in the direction of generosity, a world in which one thing never precludes another.

Later a fan spills cool air across my back, and because I'm feeling sad, my friend feeds me delicacies between gulps of wine. I think of a small culvert on the ranch that connects one irrigation ditch to another—how during high water it fills at one end and overflows at the other, so that filling and emptying become the same thing.

"To yield is to be preserved whole. To be bent is to become straight. To be hollow is to be filled. To be tattered is to be renewed. To be in want is to possess. To have plenty is to be confused," Lao Tzu wrote.

Where did June go? Now it's July. Helped friends move

cattle from one mountain pasture to another. Rode Slim, my young cutting horse. Hours go by—these are always fourteen-hour days on horseback—and suddenly he and I are in harmony and I can steer him, not with reins but with the knotted wheel of my pelvis. As we race after a cow and calf, his legs thump up into my body like pistons: I know where each foot is all the time, and he feels me in the center of him. Together we float. The reins are made of helium, his head bending, bending the way water does, following the path of least resistance; our movement is a result not of control and force but of mutual release so that the life can come up through our bodies.

None of this would be possible without a horse trainer named Ray Hunt. I go to him each summer, as much for what he teaches me about how to live as for what he can teach a horse. "You are stupid and the colt is smart," he says at the beginning of each five-day clinic. And he means it. In his sixties now, Ray, big, powerful, and weathered, grew up cowboying on ranches in northern Nevada and Idaho, riding the rough string, putting in long days. One winter he came across a stud horse named Hondu, whom nobody could ride, much less get near. Hondu hated people: he struck, bit, kicked if approached. Ray recalls: "I lay awake plenty of nights trying to figure out how to get this horse to trust me, and I knew it wasn't going to be by tying him up or hobbling him or by teaching him any lessons. Finally, I just stopped doing things to him. When I let Hondu be the teacher, we came, by trial and error, to mutual respect and trust. And when that happens, anything is possible."

The first day a young horse is brought to Ray, he is worked loose in a round corral. Standing in the middle, Ray watches the horse move and becomes a spokesman for the horse's thoughts. "You see, he doesn't know what's going to happen to him in here; he's afraid," Ray says as the colt runs, stops, dodges his head, then runs again. "But when he sees nothing bad is going to happen if he comes toward me, then he'll begin to find sanctuary in my presence." In half an hour the colt has his head in Ray's arms.

"It's amazing what a horse goes through," Ray says, rubbing the horse's head gently. "The stress . . . a human couldn't take it. You see, a horse is as pure and innocent and clean as anything you can imagine, and he wants to please."

Later he puts halters on, saddles them, and lets them run loose in an arena, and when they're used to the saddle, the riders get on, with nothing on the horse's head for control. As they step on, the horse sometimes runs off or bucks, and the riders are prohibited from doing anything that might restrain the horse. "Pretty soon he finds out that having you on his back is no different than having a mane and tail." The riders, feeling a bit helpless, get the message: that resistance and punishment communicate only a lack of trust. "Humans always want direct answers and right now. But when working with a young horse, it should be not what you want him to do but what his capabilities are. You help bring those out, that's all."

The next day, when the riders are allowed to use a snaffle bit or a hackamore, Ray admonishes us: "I try to do less and less with a horse. To give the least resistance to the life in the body and to let him stay united within himself. A horse will feel that and respond accordingly."

By the end of the five days the young horse stops, turns,

backs, has the beginnings of a sliding stop and spinning turn, and is moving in the direction of his own energy, not away from tension. "When you're riding, it should look like a bird flying," Ray says, smiling. "Not a gut-shot bird . . . it should be smooth as silk. And I'll tell you what it takes to accomplish this: self-discipline. We humans only know how to put pressure on. We're good at making war, but it's a hell of a trial for us to make peace. Peace means respond and respect, not fear and escape. I try to operate, not through pressure, but a feel. When I'm not giving, only taking, the horse starts acting out of self-preservation, and then watch out. He'll survive, but you may not."

At the end of the day he gathers his students around. The horses stand quietly. "A horse is a mirror. I know everything about you by looking at your horse," he says. Then he thumps his heart: "Dig in here. You'll be surprised at what you find. My goodness, it's amazing, when you really dig deep, what you see inside. And once you start giving, there's no end to what you get back."

August. I am camped with friends in Yellowstone Meadows, a ten-hour ride horseback through timbered mountains where, two years ago at this time, fires burned hot. This year the meadows are a wild garden thick with flowers, walled by the volcanic arms of the Yellowstone caldera. Clouds of mosquitoes rise with clouds of pollen. Early every morning I go for a walk, bear bell banging against my thigh. A stand of trees to my left is all black trunks crowned with the gray hair of charred needles and branches. On the ground, where willows burned hot, circles

of tall grass have appeared, their inflorescence like lace between my legs as I walk. . . . *Who is embracing me?*

Not far from its source below Younts Peak, the Yellowstone River is still narrow. It moves like glass, bends at
oxbows, melts into one transparency laminated onto another
as if to show me how true wealth should look.

The meadow is bombastic, a thick, bright mass of
grasses, forbs, shrubs—fescue, blue bunch, timothy, sedge,
yarrow, elk thistle, and cinquefoil, all punctuated with wildflowers of every shape—paintbrush, gentian, elephant-head,
blue penstemon, American bistort, just to name a few, and
the strange western coneflower, with its dark center and no
petals, as if, like a monk, it had shaved its head.

Pairs of sandhill cranes waddle in front of me eating
grasshoppers, then fly up, landing a little farther ahead.
Every reed-lined pool is home to families of ducks: mothers
and ducklings and protective, busybody drakes. In the larger
ponds, the beavers' dome houses look like pavilions, with
pond water as a moat. To have been made one of the animals
and to live here . . . how envious I am.

Evening.　　Allan Savory, who taught me what I know
about holistic management on our ranch, and is on this pack
trip with us, talks of growing up in the African bush. He
lived in a house with no windows or doors, and the animals—all sizes, from mosquitoes to lions—came and went.
He talks of the remarkable intelligence of animals, how one
bull giraffe, routed out by a contender, went miles away to
live. When his opponent died, ten years later, he knew and
returned to the herd. Over a sumptuous dinner of curried
rice, with beef and trout, white wine and sourdough bread,

he talks about going into the bush for months as a tracker
with only rice, tea, and a gun; how once, on a cold night,
he took shelter from rain under a dead elephant's ear, hack-
ing away at its neck for meat; how hungry he was. . . .

Morning.   Mist on the river. Two moose grazing across
the meadow, smooth as water moving. A raft of pink clouds
rises over the mountain like a wing, then sandhill cranes fly
up, their bodies the color of the sky before first light. "Karooo, karooo, karooo . . . ," their cries so deep they sound
like bells echoing off basaltic rock, carried back across moving water . . .

What is this wild embrace? This slipping away of heat
from air at daybreak, these clothes made of bird cries being
peeled from my body? *Who is holding me?* Why do your
arms keep sliding down my back and hips, then start again
at my face? What is in my throat, what have I said or
swallowed? Is it foam from the river where it collides with
pointbars and cutbanks, or the rolling *r*'s of sandhill cranes?

Lao Tzu exhorts us to listen to the world "not with
ears but with mind, not with mind but with spirit." Some
days I hear what sounds like breathing: quick inhalations
from the grass, from burnt trees, from streaming clouds, as
if desire were finally being answered, and at night in my
sleep I can feel black tree branches pressing against me, their
long needles combing my hair. Later, when the man I love
holds me, I am astonished that such an intense feeling could
come from the embrace of only one body and two hands.

Late August.   North of the ranch, I walk to stone tablets that rise three hundred feet from a steep mountain slope.

At midday they throw pointed shadows like black teeth down to me, and I climb them, slipping on rotted granite and scree. Wind-pruned shrubs punctuate the slope. Like a bear or a bird, I quench my thirst eating rose hips along the way. Then I'm at the base of the outcrop and have to tilt my head all the way back to contemplate these monoliths.

Set like false fronts, bermed in the back, a sheer drop on the side that faces the world, they are the twin bulletin boards for the cosmos, a *tabula rasa* that has pushed up from under the ground. One eroded rock looks like a pushpin. Is this the spindle on which the tablets swivel, revealing secret rooms? Are there messages pinned to the rock, ones I can't read? Small pine cones litter the ground where I'm standing, though there are no trees. Who throws them here? I wonder. And from where?

The tablets are limestone—sedimentary rock deposited like icing on top of two-billion-year-old granite by the coming and going of shallow seas. In a time of geologic violence, the granitic basement rose and tipped so that the sedimentary layer faces outward in vertical flatirons. The more fragile shales and mudstones broke away at this point, leaving much of the limestone tablets exposed. Rock that breaks when stressed is called by geologists "competent rock," and those that bend under stress, "incompetent." On the scale between "competent" and "incompetent," limestone falls somewhere in the middle.

The tablets' surface is milky. I am told it is calcium carbonate, secreted by algae and corals. Here and there chunks of maroon chert show through: a fossil record of those tiny organisms that lived and died at the bottom of a sea.

Making my way along the base of the tablets, I come on a tiny cave, an outdoor *tokonoma* or a place where a saint or a hermit might have been installed. White-throated swifts dart out from nests built in rock niches and soar over the valley, diving for insects, their sole food. If a sudden freeze hits, as it can anytime in August, these birds can go twelve days without eating, losing sixty percent of their body weight in the process. Is this the kind of fast my heart must take on?

Now the sky above me fills with birds: ravens zigzag through false fronts, then birds I can't identify fly out in slow-moving pairs. I glass them with binoculars. Is it possible these are pigeons? What are white-banded pigeons doing up here?

Rain clouds come. The sound of North Beaver Creek crescendos and softens in tidal winds, and the narrow edge of these stone shoulders take on gold at the end of the day. As clouds spread white across the sky, then drip—not with rain, but with milk—I think it must be pigeon's crop milk sputtering down, a wondrous substance belched up from the esophagus, which has more protein than mother's milk or a cow's.

We think of pigeons as being domestic creatures, but at the turn of the century passenger pigeons boasted a population of thirty billion. While watching one migration, Audubon estimated that three hundred million birds flew over his head every hour, and when they landed to rest, their colonies were often forty miles long. They are gone now, of course, hunted out of existence, so these few pairs of wild pigeons are more precious to me, odd as they seem in such an austere, windy place.

Inching my way along the base of the tablets, I stand with my nose to rock. Here, they are an open book to me, my feet toed into the spine. Fingering the jagged edge of the fracture between the two halves, I wonder if a page has been torn out. *Tabula rasa.* Is there a codex inscribed here, and if so, how can a blank be deciphered? Or is it a song too old to have words? The rock is pink, white, green, sand, nubby, and frosted. When no one is looking, I lick it and taste salt and milk.

Time for a nap. Downslope under a many-armed Engelmann's spruce. Dreams wing through my head like swifts, fast and sure, but gone in an instant. The sound of the sea and of rivers running into the sea is continuous. Here, on the ocean floor, brain coral and red sea stars thrive; vents let out juvenile water in warm streams where bacteria and tiny organisms can live. Finally, the tablets are laid to rest and lie flat. I walk on them: they are a foundation for a great house, or else I dance, and they are a table.

Awake or asleep? I don't know which. My gaze drops far below to the lake—a blue dot, as Carl Sagan says, nothing more, yet it mirrors these tablets and this mountain. For a moment the lake looks like stone and the tablets are water, then I am somewhere inside the earth and the tablets are standing in a river. I dive under them. Bubbles rise to the surface from the corner of my mouth as words. It's hot where I am, and the water is red. The tablets are anchored to the earth's molten mantle with long roots, red threads; they are teeth hung to white bone.

A song comes my way. Who is singing? Warm and cold currents carry the tune. A friend sings: "Give up your mansion of sorrow . . . I am taking it down stick by

stick . . ." Hands joined one on top of the other, like a
calf's at birth, I dive but go upward. There is no Dantean
tunnel with light at the end, no river of light in which to
paddle, only brightness narrowing to infinity. I feel as if I
had broken ribs—so hard to catch my breath. A sharp, bitter
breeze takes me by the wrists. Pale clouds unfold, revealing
flesh within flesh. Then the sky stops, but the mountain
moves like a river.

The thirteenth-century Buddhist Dōgen wrote: "Walking beyond and walking within are both done on water."
One definition of walking is to unbalance oneself by throwing a foot forward, then catching oneself with the next step.
I flounder, but around me rocks float and flower. Mountains
are made of cloud and cloud is a river lifted into the sky
and sky is water always, pulling its currents from the oceans
below. Dōgen says: "Water is the only truth of water. Water
is water's complete virtue."

I feel hands on my body. *What kind of embrace is this?*
Everything aches. Blood stings as it pumps through, con-
torted rib bones squeeze breathing. Leaning back against
the tablets is like leaning into water. Where do I break off
and where does water begin?

At the end of the day a pigeon flutters around my head,
dribbling crop milk into my mouth. *Delicious* . . . Then,
pitching out over the precipice, I pass beyond this rock-
studded mountain. So much has broken away already, there
is nothing to drink but air, nothing left to walk on but
water, yet the fasting heart grows full.